LONGMAN IMPRINT BOOK

Thrillers

selected and edited by
John Foster

with photographs by
Catherine Shakespeare Lane
assisted by Lucie Mayer

Longman Group UK Limited,
Longman House, Burnt Mill, Harlow,
Essex CM20 2JE, England
and Associated Companies throughout the world.

First published 1990
Second impression 1992

Set in 11/13 point Baskerville, Linotron 202
Printed in Malaysia by TCP

ISBN 0 582 05552 0

940780

Contents

An Introduction by Peter Lovesey

'Ready?'

I nodded nervously in the darkness. Some people carrying long candles approached and formed themselves into a procession. At the head was a figure in a vast scarlet cloak, and someone was carrying a human skull with eye sockets that glowed from some inner light. As the novice in this bizarre ceremony, I had to wait for the entire membership of the club to pass through the double doors to the room in the Café Royal where my initiation was to take place. I followed, flanked by my proposers, knowing that shortly I must place my hand on the skull and swear an oath of loyalty. They seemed to take it very seriously.

'How did I get myself into this?' I thought.

Some time previously I had seen a small advertisement in a newspaper offering a thousand pound prize for a first crime novel. Ignorant, literally clueless, about crime writing, but better informed about athletics, I had written a 'whodunit' constructed around a six-day long distance race in Victorian London. My inexperience paid off, because my plot won the prize for its originality. The publishers had asked for more crime stories.

And now I had been honoured with an invitation to join the Detection Club. I had better not divulge the details of the ceremony on the other side of the double doors. I survived. But I can let you into some secrets I learned about crime writing that were more fascinating to me than the initiation ritual. They can be valuable to anyone wanting to write a crime story.

First, the people who write them. I had always pictured crime writers as genteel old ladies or Oxford dons. True, there were one or two sweet, silver-topped ladies in the Detection Club. Agatha Christie was the President, the wearer of the scarlet cloak. And there were academics. But I also met a former chef (Len Deighton), an ex-jockey (Dick Francis), an ex-journalist (Ruth Rendell) and a former Red Cross nurse (P D James). People from many walks of life turn successfully to crime-writing.

One writer of thrillers confessed to me that he always faints at the sight of blood. Another, that she never reads other people's stories because they give her bad dreams. Without exception, they were willing to talk about the craft of crime-writing and the pleasure they got from it. Almost all of them enjoyed writing short stories as a change from novels. They encouraged me to try, so I picked up all the advice they were willing to give.

Where do crime writers get their ideas from? Anywhere they can. There is no single source of inspiration. Sometimes ideas appear to arrive from nowhere and at other times they have to be sought out. Things overheard may set the imagination working, or bits of information from books. The germ of a story may be contained in a newspaper report, or an item on television. If you are lucky, ideas can come from some personal experience or in a dream.

How do you spot a promising idea? Rarely, so far as I could discover, does it arrive complete, the perfect plot for a story. In most cases, it is no more than a flimsy mental suggestion, a fragment, a thought of 'What if...?' Once I was doing some research into family history and I happened to notice that the man next to me in the registry office was looking up the name of Smith. I thought of the problems he must have trying to trace his ancestors among the millions of Smiths and an idea dawned. When I got home I plotted a crime story, working in some twists and surprises, and it was later adapted for television in *Tales of the Unexpected*.

The idea for my story 'Fall-Out' in this collection came to me in a garden shop when I saw a display of axes of various sizes. I wondered what would happen if someone who was clearly no suburban gardener − a man of violent appearance − came into the shop to buy an axe. Would they sell him one, or call the police? Was he really violent? The idea was born.

Not all ideas come so easily. Something may occur to you that has promise, but requires some extra spark to ignite it. You can try approaching it from a different angle, perhaps putting the incident into a different setting, or with fresh characters. You may choose to speculate on what took place before, or what happens next. Most of the stories in this collection stem from simple ideas or images. The next thing to consider is how best to use the idea. The obvious way is not always the best.

I *didn't* meet Sir Arthur Conan Doyle, the creator of Sherlock Holmes, at the Detection Club, for he died before I was born, but I do know some advice he gave in his autobiography, *Memories and Adventures:* 'The first thing is to get your idea. Having got that key idea one's next task is to conceal it and lay emphasis upon everything which can make for a different explanation.' Conan Doyle was talking about plotting. When you have read a story like Ruth Rendell's *The Wrong Category* in this collection, and you know the ending, study it a second time to see how skilfully she uses Conan Doyle's method to plot her story, leading you to make quite wrong assumptions. Cathy Ace lures the reader into a trap no less ingenious in 'Dear George'.

Some writers excel at creating suspense, and the short story is well suited to the kind of plot that puts the characters into dangerous or potentially violent situations. Ray Bradbury's 'The Fruit at the Bottom of the Bowl' and John Gordon's 'Without a Mark' each concentrate on the experience of a single character under stress in the aftermath of sudden death. Guilt is a compelling theme. Notice how in each of these stories the physical description of the house contributes powerfully to the sinister atmosphere. And see how the plots build to nightmarish climaxes.

It is remarkable how many short crime stories begin *after* the crime has been committed, an observation that is worth bearing in mind if you want to plot one of your own. The guilty behaviour of the criminal, or the efforts to unmask him or her, can be more fascinating to read about than the violent act that went before. Many readers and writers of crime stories will tell you that the mere fact of a crime is unimportant. Other considerations draw them to the story: the puzzle, the suspense and the satisfaction of knowing that in most cases justice will be upheld.

Before moving on from the plot, I want to stress some variations that the short story form enables you to try. Most of us think of murder as the staple ingredient of a crime story. Sometimes full-length crime novels are simply referred to as 'murders'. A short story is an opportunity, if desired, for the writer to break the mould and feature some other crime. Marjorie Allingham plots a robbery as neat as a conjuring trick in 'The Lieabout' and Dick Francis engages our interest in a cleverly contrived racetrack fraud in 'Twenty-one Good Men and True'. Equally, you may choose to experiment with form. Because the short story is only a few pages long, you can try telling it in ways that might become strained in a full-length book. The obvious examples here are Cathy Ace's ingenious use of diary entries in 'Dear George' and Millie Murray's 'A Blessing in Disguise', written in West Indian dialect. Short stories written in the form of letters are interesting to try. I once wrote one as if through a series of questions and answers to a problem page in a women's magazine; finally, the 'agony aunt' was murdered, and the story ended with a notice to say that somebody else would take over in the next issue.

Now let's turn to the characters used in crime writing. My friends at the Detection Club might not be too pleased to hear me say that the trouble with the traditional 'whodunit' – in which murder is committed at a country house and everyone appears to be a suspect until the detective names the killer in the last chapter – is that the characters are too often cardboard-thin, dreary stereotypes. In those books the writers sometimes get so carried away by the fiendish cleverness of the puzzle that the characters are mere pawns in the game. Of course, it would not be sensible to attempt a full scale 'whodunit' as a short story. Not one of the stories in this book could be so described.

You find instead that in almost every case, the writer limits the number of main characters to four or fewer. This isn't an unbreakable rule – you can try anything – but the experienced writers in this collection seem to have found that it works best for their stories. Even Dick Francis, whose fraud story involves a team of twenty-one (in addition to the mastermind), shows us only one at work.

Given this small cast, the writer seeks to present them as individuals. This takes a little more trouble than pressing on with the plot. Indeed, the best way of conveying character is through action and dialogue in the narrative, rather than just writing a paragraph of description, detailing colour of hair, height, physical appearance, clothes and so on. Elizabeth Ferrars shows how unobtrusively, yet effectively, it can be done in the opening sequence of 'Instrument of Justice'. Her character, Frances, is plunged into the story from the first sentence. The first lines of physical description – 'a dark, angularly handsome woman of forty' – come in the second paragraph, integrated into a sentence when she is 'staring before her...possessed by a new horror.' Dramatic things are happening, and the reader is not held up by the description. The personality of Frances emerges through the way she reacts to events. She is quick-brained, resourceful and energetic. We know without being told that she is equal to every emergency.

I am not sure whether Elizabeth Ferrars based the character of Frances on somebody she knew. Writers frequently do have somebody real in mind when first putting a character on to the page. As the story develops, the character will alter and acquire an independent existence, so even if you base your portrayal on a close friend, it is unlikely that he will recognise himself. Famous characters such as Sherlock Holmes, Father Brown and George Smiley are all said to have been drawn originally from real people the authors had met and found interesting.

Having chosen your characters, you may decide that one of them should appear to tell the story in his or her own words, in the first person, as Marjorie Allingham and John Gordon do in this collection. This can help to achieve immediacy, the feeling that the reader is closer to the events. John Gordon's narrator in 'Without a Mark' is a thirteen-year-old. The writer makes this believable not only through the action, but by the use of language within the compass of a literate boy of that age. If you take an identity, you must sustain it convincingly.

A single character can dominate the plot in another way, notably when his or her personality becomes so domineering or obsessive that it dictates the outcome of the story. Ruth Rendell's character Della, in the ironically titled story 'You Can't Be Too Careful', is interesting to compare with Ray Bradbury's William Acton, in 'The Fruit at the Bottom of the Bowl'. Each behaves as most of us would, to a point. Both go far beyond that point, towards self-destruction.

Ideas, plot and character are all crucial elements in story-writing, but there is something else that I must not neglect to mention, for it is vital. As a candle-carrying member of the Detection Club, I sometimes look at my fellow-members and wonder whether they have *anything* in common, apart from the ability to spell. Their age ranges from twenty-something to eighty-something. They include writers of every sort of crime fiction from the traditional 'whodunit' to the contemporary spy thriller. Can there be anything that accounts for their success in having books published? I think there is one factor, and that is that they *enjoy* their writing. To be successful, you must write to please yourself. It should be exciting and satisfying. If it is, you will convey it to the reader.

I am confident that you will enjoy the stories in this collection. I wish you joy in your writing.

Peter Lovesey

Fall-Out

'I need an axe.'

Everyone in the garden shop turned to look at the man who needed an axe. He was not dressed like the other customers in blue and beige gabardine jackets and creased trousers. He was in a string vest and faded jeans. His long, blond hair was drawn back and fixed behind his neck with a leather bootlace. He had a silver earring. And around his neck a string of wooden beads.

Mr Padmore, the shop owner, believed in giving all his customers the same courteous service. He had not served the man before, but he had sometimes seen him passing up the street. 'An axe, sir? I think you'll find a good selection here. The size you have depends on the job you need it for.'

'How much is that one?'

'The big one? Beautiful to handle, and razor sharp. Twenty-one fifty.'

The man picked it up and felt the weight. He put his two hands on the shaft and raised it. For one petrifying moment, Mr Padmore thought he was about to bring it crashing down on a display of ornamental plaster animals. Instead he let the length of the shaft slip through his hands and examined the head.

'I'll take it.'

He placed the axe on the counter and took a wad of crumpled banknotes from his back pocket.

Mr Padmore grinned companionably. 'Shall I wrap

it? You might get arrested carrying it through the street.'

'No need. I live just around the corner.'

'Really?' said Mr Padmore as he checked the money. 'I ought to know you, then.'

'You wouldn't. I haven't been in here before.' He gave Mr Padmore a steady look with his pale blue eyes. 'I'm not interested in gardening. I hate it.'

Mr Padmore was so anxious not to provoke a scene in his shop that he practically agreed that he, too, hated gardening. 'It's a heavy commitment. No end of work. No joy in it unless you're dedicated.' He added knowingly, 'Nothing like a good, old-fashioned log fire to get you through the winter.'

The man who needed an axe stared back at him.

Mr Padmore explained, 'I thought you wanted it for chopping firewood.'

'No.' The man picked the axe off the counter and walked out of the shop.

When the door closed, Mr Padmore said, to break the tension, 'What else could he want it for, except to chop his neighbours into little pieces?' He turned to his next customer, who was wearing tweeds, and wanted hyacinth bulbs.

On the far side of the display of garden furniture in the centre of the shop, one of Mr Padmore's regular customers was in a state of shock. Gilbert Crawshaw happened to be the next-door neighbour of the man who had bought the axe. He had twitched with horror at Mr Padmore's last remark.

Crawshaw was tall, which was an asset, with a narrow build, which was not. He had grey hair and black-framed bifocals. He was fifty-one, and he worked in the treasurer's department at County Hall, where his status was senior clerical officer. But if his career had not been notably successful, he had the consolation of a marriage which was in every way satisfactory to him. Joan understood him, cared for his house, cooked well and was ten years younger than he, which was good for his self-esteem.

Theirs was a council house in Jubilee Road, a pleasant street in a good locality, close to the shops and surrounded by a private housing development that the estate agents described as exclusive and sought after. Crawshaw had qualified for a council house because of his job at County Hall, and he had made sure that the house he got was in Jubilee Road. He liked to think that he had helped to set the standard that made it harmonise with the gracious streets of private housing.

His fastidiously tidy garden typified his life. There was a square lawn surrounded with herbaceous border plants that he bought each spring at Mr Padmore's and planted in the same regularly spaced arrangement. No weeds grew there. No slugs skulked under leaves. The garden was sprayed and fed with recommended products from the shop.

It had been a shock for Crawshaw eight months earlier when the new people had moved in next door. The old couple they replaced had lived there over thirty years – quiet, decent people who minded their own business and didn't keep animals. Towards the end they had tended to let the garden go and turn up the volume on the television, but you had to make allowances for old age.

These new ones – their name was Stock, or *his* was, at any rate – were disquieting in quite another respect. They had arrived in a Transit van one Sunday morning with several friends, similarly long-haired and sandalled. Crawshaw had been trimming the privet in the front. He had gone inside to watch from behind the net curtains in the spare bedroom. His first suspicion was that they were squatters. All the furniture they possessed had travelled in the back of that small van. It included two mattresses and several cushions, but no bed. There were also a number of indoor plants of a type he had never seen in the garden shop.

The next day, Crawshaw had called into the housing department across the corridor from his office to check whether the house had yet been allocated. That was how he had learned that the man's name was Stock. He was now the lawful occupant. He had been given the house because he was homeless and unemployed and his wife was six months pregnant.

'His wife?' Crawshaw had repeated. 'I may be mistaken, but I don't think she wears a wedding ring.'

'Wife, common law wife, we make no distinction these days,' the woman in housing had explained. 'You and I may not approve, Mr Crawshaw, but those are our instructions.'

That evening, Crawshaw told his wife Joan what he had learned.

'I know,' she told him. 'I met them this afternoon.'

Joan had a quiet style of speech that Crawshaw usually found congenial, but occasionally she shocked him. He was never certain from her mild expression whether she meant to shock.

'*Met* them?'

'I baked some cakes and took them round. You have to be neighbourly, Gilbert. They invited me in for a coffee.'

'You went in?'

'Yes,' Joan answered matter-of-factly. 'Poor dears, they haven't any chairs yet, so I sat on a cushion on the floor. They're really quite sweet.'

'You shouldn't have done it,' Crawshaw told her.

'Sometimes I despair of you, Joan. We don't know what sort of people they are.'

'We never will, if you have your way,' she pointed out.

Crawshaw's usually pale face turned purple. 'Joan, I forbid you, I absolutely forbid you to make any more overtures to Stock and his woman.'

He had never spoken to her like that in their fifteen years of married life, and it stunned her into silence.

In the months since then, Crawshaw had noticed other disturbing developments. There had been parties. He had counted as many as fifty-six guests on one occasion and some of them had stayed all night. He knew because he had counted everyone who had left. About one-thirty, the music had stopped and there were still at least a dozen in the house. He was sure that if there was no music, sinister things were going on. Joan told him to be grateful for the chance to get some sleep, but he was quite unable to relax.

One evening in the summer, Crawshaw had decided to walk home through the park instead of taking his customary route down Mason's Lane and along the High Street. It had meant using the subway to cross the railway. Halfway through the tunnel, his thoughts had been disturbed by the sound of a woman singing. Her voice had a clear tone that Crawshaw found quite pleasant until he noticed who she was and who was the person accompanying her on a guitar.

They were the people from next door.

She had the baby slung in front of her on a harness and was standing beside Stock, who was sitting on the stone floor with a wooden bowl between his feet to collect coins thrown by passers-by. Stock actually nodded to Crawshaw as he moved stiffly past them without putting his hand anywhere near his pocket.

'Can you imagine how I felt?' he asked Joan when he got home. 'Our neighbours, for heaven's sake, begging for money in a public thoroughfare.'

'It's not really begging,' Joan commented.

'That's what it amounts to.'

'Well, at least it's not dishonest.'

'It's degrading. How would you feel if I stood in the subway strumming a guitar?'

'Certainly surprised and probably elated, if you really want to know,' Joan answered, more to herself than her husband.

It didn't matter, because Crawshaw wasn't listening. He said, 'I think the social security people ought to be told. Stock has no right to public hand-outs if he has an income of his own.'

'Gilbert, let it rest,' Joan urged.

He did not. The next morning, before the office was open to the public, he saw the senior administrative officer in the social security wing. She said she was grateful for the information and they would ask Stock about it next time he came in, but these casual earnings were impossible to assess with accuracy. Crawshaw challenged this assumption. He said it was no good tamely asking Stock for information. It should be the subject of a departmental investigation. He went on to mention the parties. 'I counted fifty-six guests. Anyone with the means to entertain on that scale should not be living off the state.'

The senior administrative officer said she would do all she reasonably could to see that Mr Stock was not defrauding the department, but Crawshaw heard no more about it.

That is, until the incident in the garden shop.

'I tell you, he bought an axe,' he told Joan as soon as he got back, 'and Padmore said it was obvious what he wanted it for – to attack the neighbours.'

'He must have been joking, Gilbert.'

'What sort of joke is that? I don't find it funny.'

Joan sighed and shook her head. 'People are not very tolerant. The Stocks dress differently from most of us, so it gives rise to silly comments. It's a basic instinct, a tribal thing.'

Crawshaw sniffed. 'I don't need you to tell me that. I can recognise a couple of savages for myself.'

'Gilbert, that's unworthy of you. I took you for a tolerant man.'

'Not much use being tolerant when there's someone coming at you with an axe.'

'Now you're being melodramatic. What have we ever done to antagonise Mr Stock?'

Crawshaw turned his head and stared out of the window. He hadn't mentioned his conversation with the senior administrative officer in social security. Joan had tried to discourage him from reporting on the neighbours. It was no use talking to her about social duty. She hadn't progressed beyond the morality of the playground, when 'telling' was a crime.

Yet he was beginning to wish he hadn't interfered.

No more was said on the matter until mid-afternoon, when Crawshaw was in the garden mowing his lawn. He favoured the conventional mower with a roller that left a pleasing pattern of stripes. He had sometimes looked at the rotary mowers in Padmore's shop, but they didn't give the same finish. It was while he was making his journeys up and down the lawn that he heard a sound above the whirr of the mower. He thought at first that a stone had lodged between the blades, but when he stopped, the sound persisted. It was coming from the next garden, a knock as steady as a steam-hammer.

There was a six-foot fence between the gardens, so he had to go indoors and upstairs to see what was happening.

Joan was already in the spare bedroom watching. 'You see?' she said, as he joined her at the curtain. 'I told you there was nothing to get alarmed about.'

Crawshaw stared down at the spectacle of his neighbour Stock hacking with the axe at the only tree in his garden.

He said, 'Disgusting.'

'Oh, come, Gilbert,' said Joan. 'It's a stifling afternoon and that's warm work. A man is entitled to take off his shirt in the privacy of his own garden. It's in no way offensive.'

'I can see it doesn't offend *you*,' Crawshaw commented pointedly.

Joan coloured and said, 'What do you mean?'

'If you really want to know,' Crawshaw said with condescension in his voice, 'I wasn't speaking about his naked torso when I used the word "disgusting". Obviously that sprang to your mind first. What I had in mind was the destruction of that apple tree, which I regard as an act of senseless vandalism. That tree is the last beautiful thing in their neglected garden, and there he is destroying it.'

Joan was silent, nursing her private hurt.

'If it falls against our fence,' Crawshaw went on, 'he'll be hearing from my solicitor.'

Joan said, 'At least we know why he bought the axe.' She waited for some response and, getting none, added, 'He wasn't planning to attack you.'

'I'm going down to finish the lawn,' said Crawshaw. 'No, there's no need for you to come. You carry on goggling at the ape-man.'

'That's unfair, Gilbert,' Joan said, but he was already on his way downstairs.

A short while later, Crawshaw looked up from his mowing and saw the top of the apple tree shudder and lurch. He stopped to watch which way it fell. There was no damage to his fence. The tree fell the other way.

He still said, 'Vandal,' before resuming his work. Later, he was obliged to go indoors. Stock had started a bonfire to burn the tree. Smoke was billowing across Crawshaw's garden.

'That's green wood,' he told Joan as they stood in the bedroom watching. 'It's not fit for burning. It'll smoke out the entire neighbourhood. The man has no consideration for other people.'

During that week, Stock made more bonfires, generally in the evening when Crawshaw was home from work. By sheer persistence, the wood was reduced to ashes by the weekend.

Crawshaw called at the garden shop on Saturday. He needed something to treat a patch of moss which had appeared on his lawn. Mr Padmore selected a packet from the shelves behind the counter and handed it to Crawshaw.

'That should do the trick,' he told him. 'One sachet to a gallon of water. Funny you should come in, Mr Crawshaw. We were talking about you earlier this morning.'

'In what connection?' Crawshaw asked uneasily.

'Nothing personal. That neighbour of yours came in. Long-haired chap. He *does* live next door to you, doesn't he?'

Crawshaw nodded.

'That was how your name came up,' said Mr Padmore.

'Did *he* mention it?'

Mr Padmore's mouth gave nothing away, but his eyes glittered artfully. 'Don't you two get on very well?' he asked.

'We don't have much in common,' Crawshaw guardedly answered.

'I can see that, Mr Crawshaw, I can see that.'

Crawshaw didn't altogether like Padmore's tone, but curiosity kept him from cutting the conversation short. He remarked, 'I can't think what my neighbour would want from this shop. He hasn't shown any interest in his garden in the time he's lived there.'

'He bought a spade,' said Mr Padmore. 'Last week it was an axe.' He winked at Crawshaw. 'You keep an eye on him, Mr Crawshaw.'

'Why?'

'It's obvious, isn't it? What does he want with a spade if he doesn't go in for gardening? He must be planning to bury something.'

When Crawshaw got home, he told Joan precisely what Mr Padmore had said.

'And you took it seriously?' she said. 'Gilbert, what's the matter with you?'

'There's nothing the matter with me.'

'You must have a persecution complex, or something.'

Crawshaw reached out and gripped her by the arms so tightly that she gave a cry of pain. He said, 'Listen to me, will you? If anyone is behaving oddly, it's that blighter next door. You won't find me scrounging off social security, or squatting in the subway with a begging bowl between my legs. I don't hack down healthy fruit trees and pollute the atmosphere with filthy bonfires. Just think of that before you try your pseudo-psychology on me.'

'Gilbert, you're hurting me,' said Joan.

That afternoon they watched Stock use the spade to dig out the stump of the apple tree.

'Are you satisfied?' Joan asked.

Crawshaw didn't answer, so she went downstairs and put on the television.

The next morning, she was surprised to find when she woke that her husband was not in bed. She checked the time and found that it was not yet 8 a.m. It was Crawshaw's invariable custom on Sunday mornings to remain in bed until 8.15 a.m., when the papers came. Joan drew on her housecoat, sensing that something disturbing had occurred.

She found him in the spare bedroom, staring out of the window, his back and shoulders rigid with tension.

'What is it, Gilbert?'

He said in a low voice that she scarcely heard, 'See for yourself.'

She stood at his side and looked down into the garden next door. There was no one there. There was just the hole where the stump of the apple tree had been. It had been shaped and extended into a rectangular shaft about seven feet in length and three feet wide. It was at least five feet deep.

'There must be an explanation,' said Joan.

'It's a grave,' whispered Crawshaw.

'It can't be,' said Joan. 'Let's get some breakfast.'

But Crawshaw remained where he was. Joan made some coffee and took it to him, but he didn't drink it. Nor did he speak to her.

Down below, Stock had resumed his digging.

By eleven, Joan had decided to talk to the woman next door. As a pretext, she found some soft wool left over from a jacket she had knitted for her niece's baby. She took it round and offered it for their child.

The woman was very appreciative. She invited Joan in for coffee. When it was made, she called Mr Stock in from the garden. Without Joan having to enquire, he explained what he was doing.

When Joan went back to her house, Crawshaw was still at the window in the spare bedroom. He was still in his dressing gown. He hadn't even noticed that she had gone next door.

'It's not what you think,' she told him gently. 'I've been talking to them. They are very concerned about the prospect of a nuclear war. Mr Stock is building a fall-out shelter.'

Crawshaw said nothing then. Nearly an hour later, when Joan was putting the beef joint into the oven, she heard his voice behind her. She almost dropped the tin in surprise.

He said, 'It's idiotic, trying to build a nuclear shelter.'

'Possibly,' conceded Joan, 'but it shows a pleasing regard for the safety of his wife and child. They say it should be big enough for us as well if we care to share it with them.'

'He won't get any help from me, if that's what he's after.'

'I'm sure he doesn't expect it,' said Joan.

Later, over lunch, Crawshaw said, 'I don't suppose he got planning permission for this.'

'Does it matter?'

'Of course it matters. You can't build things like that without clearing it first with the council. There are pipes and cables and heaven knows what buried underground. There's also the danger of subsidence. He might undermine the foundations of my house.'

'Gilbert, let's talk about something else.'

'Not until I've settled this. Tomorrow morning, I want you to go to the borough surveyor's department and find out whether Stock obtained the necessary planning permission.'

'You want me to go? Why me?'

'Because they know me at the council. You needn't give your name. Everyone is entitled to look at the list.'

'Then why don't you do it yourself?'

'I didn't tell you before, but you might as well know now that I reported them to social security. For all the good it did, I might as well have saved myself the trouble, but you see that I don't want it thought that I have a grudge against the neighbours.'

'You don't want it known,' said Joan quietly.

Crawshaw put down his knife and fork and said in a low voice that she found more menacing than a shout, 'You will do as I say. If you choose to defy me, you must suffer the consequences.'

He had frightened her. There had been no violence in their marriage, but she knew him well enough to fear the force of retribution in his character. She knew better than to rouse it.

Next morning, she did as he instructed. She went to the borough surveyor's department and enquired whether there was planning permission for a nuclear fall-out shelter at 9 Jubilee Road. To her amazement and relief, the clerk confirmed that there was. He got out the detailed plan for Joan to examine. It had the council stamp on it, and the signature of the borough surveyor.

She thought that her morning's work would bring reassurance to her husband, but she should have known better. When she told him that evening, he accepted the information with a shrug and went upstairs to take another look at the excavations.

Through that summer, Crawshaw kept vigil for hours on end in the spare bedroom. Joan rarely saw him except when it was too dark to stare out of the window. Their own garden began to show signs of neglect. Daisies and dandelions flourished on the lawn. The flowerbeds dried out in the warm spell at the end of August.

Joan often spoke to the people next door. She always found them friendly. They told her that the shelter would be ready before the winter. The main chamber was complete. There was still construction work inside, to fit it out and make it habitable.

One evening in October, Crawshaw came downstairs and said, 'You've been talking to them again, haven't you?'

Joan answered, 'There's no law against it, Gilbert. They *are* our neighbours. And you must admit I don't get much conversation with you these days.'

He ignored that. 'What's happening with the shelter?'

'Well, if you don't know, I'm sure I don't.'

'He's working underground now. I can't see what he's doing.'

'How maddening for you.'

'Don't be provocative, Joan. You've been talking to them. Tell me what's going on.'

'Why don't you ask them yourself? It wouldn't hurt to exchange a few civil words, Gilbert. They're very approachable people.'

He glared at her, and said no more. She felt for the first time in months that she had won a point.

One evening later in the week, he asked, 'Is the digging finished?'

Joan looked up and answered mildly, 'I haven't enquired.'

'Have you looked inside? Have they shown it to you?'

'Gilbert, I'm not interested in looking inside their

shelter. I'm sure Mr Stock would be delighted to show it to you if you asked him.'

'I think he's still extending it,' said Crawshaw. 'He wouldn't want me to see it.'

'Oh, that's it, is it? You think he's burrowing like a mole. Under the fence and under our garden? Perhaps that's why our clematis died.'

Crawshaw's eyes widened. 'Has it?'

Joan was not sure what had prompted her to mention the clematis. She knew she was making mischief. The combination of a baking sun and the lack of any watering had killed the clematis. Gilbert had not even noticed its demise, but he would seize on it as evidence of subterranean invasion.

He took the next day off from work, something he had never done in his life, apart from a few days for illness. By 8 a.m., he was out there with his spade and wheelbarrow. Joan supposed at first that he intended catching up on the backlog of weeding, but it was soon apparent that he was otherwise engaged.

He was digging a hole.

He had started in the flowerbed where the dead clematis was, beside the fence separating their garden from the Stocks'. By lunchtime, the hole had developed into a trench. By mid-afternoon, the trench extended along the length of the fence. Plants and young trees that Crawshaw had tended for years were dug out and left to wither on the piles of topsoil and clay. He was working like a man possessed.

About 4 p.m., Joan went out to him and said, 'Gilbert, you're destroying our garden.'

Crawshaw carried on digging. He was chest-deep in the trench. 'Better than having it destroyed by someone else.'

'What are you doing this for?'

'To find where the damned shelter comes out.'

'It isn't in our garden, Gilbert.'

'It is. You'll see.'

'I saw the plans,' said Joan.

'Plans!' said Crawshaw, spitting into his trench.

Joan looked up at the house next door and noticed Mr and Mrs Stock standing at their bedroom window staring down at them. They didn't have net curtains. She ran indoors.

Crawshaw didn't come in from the garden until after eight. By then it was dark, and raining, and the wet mud was gleaming on his clothes and body. He was standing in the kitchen doorway holding out a plug attached to a length of cable. 'Plug that in, would you?'

'You're not carrying on with this?' said Joan in disbelief.

'It's dark. I need a lamp.'

'You'll get pneumonia.'

'Do as I tell you. I haven't time to stand here talking.'

She sighed, took the plug and pressed it into the socket. 'Why, Gilbert? At least tell me why.'

He laughed.

It was so unusual for him to laugh that Joan found it no comfort at all.

Crawshaw said smuggly, 'I've found it. I've found the top edge of his infernal shelter projecting nearly three feet into our garden. I knew I'd find it if I went deep enough. And now I'm going to attack it with a sledge and crowbar. It might withstand a nuclear blast, but it won't stop me from exercising my rights as the lawful tenant of this land. Do you want to try and stop me?'

Joan answered quietly, 'You must do as you think fit, Gilbert.'

As soon as he had gone, she went out through the front and knocked on the Stocks' door. Mr Stock opened it. He said, 'You look as if you could do with a drink.'

He invited her in. They were very kind to her. They produced a glass of sherry. She was grateful. She explained about the digging and said, 'Gilbert says he has found something. He's convinced that it must be your shelter.'

Mr Stock shook his head. 'Impossible. It stops at least five feet our side of the fence. There's nothing underground on your side except the conduit for the main electric cable. I saw the plans. God, if he cuts through that...' He got up and went to the window, but before he reached it, the lights went out.

In the garden next door, the lights had gone out for ever for Gilbert Crawshaw.

And in the darkness of the Stocks' living room, Joan Crawshaw permitted herself a sigh. No one else could have noticed that it was more a sigh of relief than regret. She was free.

She, too, had taken note of those plans.

Instrument of Justice
Elizabeth Ferrars

Elizabeth Ferrars

Instrument of Justice

When Frances Liley read in the obituary column of
The Times of the death of Oliver Darnell, beloved husband of Julia, suddenly at his home, she folded her
arms on the table before her, put her head down on
them and burst into violent tears. Anyone who had seen
her then would have assumed that she was weeping at
the loss of a dear friend. In fact, they were tears of
relief, healing and wonderful. At last she was free. No
threat hung over her any more. Or so she thought until
she had had time to do a little thinking.

As soon as she had she sat back abruptly, dried her
eyes roughly and sat staring before her, a dark, angularly handsome woman of forty, possessed by a new horror.
For when a person died his solicitor or his executors or
someone would have to go through his papers and
somewhere they would find those terrible photographs.
And God knew what would happen then. At least with
Oliver, Frances had known where she was. Two
thousand a year to him, which it had not been too
difficult for her to find, and she had been relatively safe.
But if someone else found the photographs and felt
inclined to send them to Mark, her husband, he would
immediately go ahead with the divorce that he wanted
and would certainly get custody of their two children.
That would be intolerable. She must think and think
fast.

Luckily she had always had a quick brain. After only

a few minutes she knew what to do, or at least what was worth trying. Telephoning Julia Darnell, she said, 'It's Frances, Julia. I've just seen the news about Oliver. I'm so terribly sorry. I can hardly believe it. It was his heart, was it? There was always something the matter with it, wasn't there? Listen, my dear, please be quite honest with me, but would you like me to come down? I mean, if you're alone now and I can help in any way. But don't say you'd like me to come if you'd sooner I didn't. Of course I'll come to the funeral, but I could come straight away and stay on for a few days, unless you've some other friend with you.'

Julia was tearfully grateful. She had no relations of her own and had never liked Oliver's, and though the neighbours, she said, had been very kind, she was virtually alone. And she and Frances were such very old friends, she could think of no one who could help so much to break the dreadful new loneliness of bereavement. Of course Julia had never known of her husband's brief adultery with Frances, or that he had supplemented his not very large income as a painter of very abstract pictures with a sideline in blackmail, and her affection for Frances was uncomplicated and sincere. Promising to arrive that afternoon, Frances telephoned Mark in his office to tell him what had happened and that she would probably be away for a few days. The children were no problem, because they were away at their boarding school. Packing a suitcase, she set off for the Darnell's cottage in Dorset.

By that time she had a plan of sorts in her mind. On the morning of the funeral she intended to wake up with what she would claim was a virus and say that she was feeling too ill to go out. Then, during the one time when she could be certain the cottage would be empty, she would make a swift search of it for the photographs.

The probability was that they were somewhere in Oliver's studio, a very private place in which Julia had never been allowed to touch anything, even to do a little cautious dusting. If they were not there, of course, if, for instance, Oliver had kept them in the bank, then there was nothing for Frances to do but go home and wait for the worst to happen, but with luck, she thought, she would find them.

Unfortunately her plan was wrecked by the fact that on the morning of the funeral it was Julia who woke up with a virus. She had a temperature of a hundred and two, complained of a sore throat and could only speak in a husky whisper. Frances called the doctor who gave Julia some antibiotics and said that she must certainly stay in bed and not to go out into the chill of the February morning, even to attend her husband's funeral. Julia, with bright spots of fever on her plump, naturally pale cheeks, cried bitterly and said, 'But all those people coming back here to lunch, Frances – what *am* I to do about them? I can't possibly put them off now.'

For Julia had insisted that Oliver's relations, who were coming from a distance, and such neighbours as were kind enough to come to the funeral, must be given lunch in her house after it, and she and Frances had spent most of the day before assembling cold meats, salads, cheeses and a supply of rather inferior white wine for what Frances felt would be a gruesome little party, but the thought of which seemed to comfort Julia.

Again thinking fast, Frances said, 'Don't worry. I'll look after them for you. I'll go to the service, but I won't go on to the cemetery, I'll come straight back from the church and have everything ready for your friends when they arrive. Now just stay quiet and I'll look after everything.'

She gave Julia the pills that the doctor had left for her and also brought her a mug of hot milk into which she had emptied two capsules of sodium amytal which she had found in the bathroom cabinet. They would almost certainly ensure that Julia would be asleep by the time that Frances returned from the church, and though she would not have as long for her search as she had hoped, she might still be fortunate.

There were not many people in the church. A man sitting next to Frances, who started a low-voiced conversation with her before the coffin had been brought in or the vicar appeared, introduced himself as Major Sowerby and said that his wife was desperately sorry not to be able to attend, but she was in bed with a virus.

'There's a terrible lot of it around in the village,' he said. 'Is it true poor Mrs Darnell's laid up with it too?'

'I'm afraid so,' Frances said.

'Tragic for her. Most upsetting. She and Oliver were so devoted to one another. Of course I didn't understand his painting, but Isobel, my wife, who knows a lot more about that sort of thing than I do, says he deserved much more recognition than he ever had. Great dedication, she says, and such integrity.'

'Oh, complete,' Frances agreed with a sweet, sad smile, and thought that in its way it was true. Oliver had been dedicated to exploiting any woman who had been fool enough to be charmed by his astonishing good looks and to trust him. As soon as the service was over she hurried out of the church, leaving the other mourners to go on to the cemetery, and made her way along the lane that led to the Darnells' cottage.

As she entered it, she stood still, listening. All was quiet. So it looked as if the sodium amytal had done its work and Julia was asleep. But just to make sure, Frances went to the foot of the stairs and called softly, 'Julia!'

There was no reply. She waited a moment, then wrenched off her coat, dropped it on a chair and went swiftly along the passage to Oliver's studio. Presently she would have to attend to the setting out of the lunch for Julia's guests, but the search must come first. Opening the door of the studio, she went in and only then understood the reason for the quiet in the house. Julia, in her dressing-gown, was lying in the middle of the floor with her head a terrible mass of blood and with a heavy hammer on the floor beside her.

Frances was not an entirely hard-hearted person. Also, she was by nature law-abiding. Her first impulse, as she stared at the battered thing on the floor, was to call the police. But then a habit that she had of having second thoughts asserted itself. It was still of desperate importance to her to find the photographs and once the police were in the house she would have no further chance of searching for them. That made the situation exceedingly complex. For one thing, how were the police to know that it had not been Frances whom Julia, drugged and half-asleep, had heard downstairs in her husband's studio, and coming downstairs to investigate, been killed by her for it? If Frances called the police now, she thought, she might find herself in deep trouble.

But if she did not and searched for the photographs first, she would presently find herself with a cooling body on her hands and sooner or later would have to explain why she had failed to report it a few hours earlier. It did not help that she was almost certain that she knew who the murderer was. A virus can be a very convenient thing, and Mrs Sowerby, who had not attended the church, would not have found out that Julia was ill and would have assumed that the house was empty. Looking round the studio, where drawers had been pulled out and papers, letters, sketches, note-books spilled on the floor, Frances wondered if the woman had found the photographs or letters that Oliver had presumably been holding over her before she committed murder, or if she was still in terror that someone else would find them. But even if she were, she was unlikely to come back for the present, knowing that a dozen guests would shortly be arriving. Taking the key out of the door, locking it on the outside and putting the key into the pocket of the suit that she was wearing, Frances went out to the kitchen to go on with preparing the lunch.

She took all the things that she and Julia had made the day before out of the refrigerator, spooned the various salads, the prawns with rice and peppers, the cucumbers in sour cream, the coleslaw and the rest, into cut glass bowls, arranged the slices of cold turkey, meat loaf and ham on dishes, and set them out on the table in the dining-room. She put silver and wine glasses on the table and drew the corks of several of the bottles of wine. The meal was only just ready when the first guests arrived.

They were the vicar, Arthur Craddock, and his wife. He was a slender, quiet-looking man whose voice, as he recited the psalms that Julia had chosen and described Oliver's improbable virtues, had seemed unexpectedly vibrant and authoritative. But any authority that he might achieve when he was performing his professional duties was sadly diminished, in a mere social setting, by his wife, a large, hearty woman who looked kindly, but accustomed to domination and who upset Frances at once by saying that she would just pop upstairs to have a few words with poor Julia, tell her how splendidly everything had gone off and how much she had been missed.

'But the infection,' Frances stammered. 'I believe it's all round the village and I know she wouldn't want you to be exposed to it here.'

'I'm never ill,' Mrs Craddock replied. 'Ask my husband. We were in India for a time, you know, and I've nursed patients through bubonic plague and never a whit the worse. I'm sure I could give Julia a little comfort.'

'Well, later, perhaps,' Frances said, recovering her presence of mind. 'I went up to see her myself a few minutes ago and found her asleep. The doctor gave her a sedative. He said rest was what she needed, and I'm sure he's right. I know she hasn't slept properly for days. But she's looking very peaceful now, so I don't think we should disturb her.'

'Ah, no, of course not,' Mrs Craddock agreed. 'Was that Dr Bolling? Excellent man. The best type of good, old-fashioned family doctor whom you can really trust.'

She let herself and her husband be shepherded into the dining-room and they had each just accepted a glass of wine when the doorbell rang again and Frances left them to admit the next guests.

They were a brother and a cousin of Oliver's, both of whom, he had once told Frances, he knew disliked him. The next to arrive was Major Sowerby and gradually the dining-room filled, the hushed tones in which everyone spoke on first arriving rising by degrees until the noise in the room resembled that of any ordinary cocktail party. The food on the table was eaten with appetite, the wine was drunk, and the atmosphere became one of what seemed to Frances a faintly gruesome hilarity, quelled only now and again by guilt when someone was tactless enough to remind the others that these were funeral baked meats that they were consuming.

Slightly flushed, Oliver's brother remarked, 'Julia was always a jolly good cook. Pity she can't be with us now.'

'She must have taken a great deal of trouble over this,' Mrs Craddock said, 'but I expect it was good for her, taking her mind off her sorrow. I'd like to take a little of it up to her and tell her how we've all been thinking of her, because with all the noise we've been making I'm sure she must be awake by now. I'll just pop up with a plateful, shall I, and perhaps a glass of wine?'

'That's the ticket,' Major Sowerby said, 'though whisky might do her more good. I took a good strong whisky up to my wife before I left for the church, and a sandwich. She said a sandwich was all she could face. Actually I had to insist on her staying in bed, she was so upset at not being able to make it to the funeral, but obviously she wasn't fit to go out. The fact is, you know, she thought a lot of Oliver. Sat for her portrait to him once, then made me buy the thing. Well, I didn't mind doing it really, because no one could guess it's Isobel, it's all squares and triangles and she says it's good and she knows far more about that sort of thing than I do.'

Mrs Craddock was spooning prawns and rice on to a plate, murmuring, 'I wonder if she likes cucumber – it disagrees with some people,' adding a slice of turkey, a small piece of ham and reaching for a bottle of wine to fill a glass for Julia.

Frightened beyond words and desperate, Frances snatched the plate and the glass from the woman's hands, said brusquely, 'I'll take them,' made for the door and while Mrs Craddock was still only looking startled at her rudeness, shot up the stairs and through the open door into Julia's bedroom.

In its silence she first began to feel the real horror of the situation. Here she was with food and wine in her hands for a woman who lay in a room downstairs with her body cooling and her head battered in. Her gaze held hypnotised by the sight of the empty bed with its dented pillows and its blankets thrown back, Frances gulped down the wine, wishing that it was something stronger, then went downstairs again and put down the plate of untouched food on the dining-table.

'She drank the wine, but she wouldn't eat anything,' she said to Mrs Craddock. 'I gave her another of the pills the doctor left for her. She's very sleepy. I really think it's best to leave her alone.'

Frustrated in her desire to do good, the vicar's wife soon left, sweeping her husband along with her, and after that, one by one, the other guests departed. At last the house was empty and quiet again.

Too quiet, too desolate. The last hour had been the worst nightmare that Frances had ever lived through, but at least the crowd of chattering people had been a defence against thought. Now she could not escape from it any longer. There was the problem of the photographs and the problem of the corpse in the studio. Looking at the table littered with china, wine glasses and left-overs, she had an absurd idea that she might do the washing-up before trying to cope with the murder, but recognising this for the idiocy that it was, and that her motive was only to put off doing what she must, she poured out a glass of whisky, sat down at the head of the table and tried to concentrate.

The photographs came first. She must nerve herself to go back into the studio and search for them. What she did next would depend to some extent on whether or not she found them. She could hardly bear to face the possibility that she might not. With the dreadful things in his hands, Mark would certainly be able to obtain custody of the children when he went ahead with the divorce that he wanted, and she would never submit to that. For apart from the pleasure that she took in the two dear girls, it would be intolerable to let Mark triumph over her.

She thought of the photographs, of which Oliver had only once allowed her a glimpse, of how appallingly revealing they were, and of the bitter amusement with which Mark would view them. They were, in their way, superb photographs. Oliver might not have been an outstanding painter, but as a photographer he had been highly skilled, as well as incredibly ingenious. She had had no suspicion of the presence of the camera in the room at the time when he had taken the pictures, and when he had told her how he had done it, she had almost had to laugh, it had been so clever. But now she must get them back. That was what she must do before she thought of anything else.

She went back into the studio. It was easier than she had thought that it would be to disregard Julia's body, the darkening blood and the murderous hammer. Locking the door in case anyone, that well-meaning busybody, Mrs Craddock, for instance, should think of coming back, she began on a methodical search of the drawers and cupboards. To her surprise, she found the photographs almost at once, not merely prints, but the negatives too, in a box in a cupboard which she thought had not yet been opened by the previous searcher.

She found several other photographs of a similar character. Feeling dizzy with relief, close to bursting into tears as she had when she had first read of Oliver's death, she studied these, which were of three women, and wondered which of them was of Isobel Sowerby. Frances knew nothing about her except that her husband did not think that she looked as if she consisted of squares and triangles. But none of the women did. They all had more curves than angles. And two of them looked rather young to be married to Major Sowerby, though that was not the sort of thing about which it was ever possible to be sure. Men of sixty sometimes married girls in their teens. However, Frances thought that Julia's murderess was probably the third woman, who was about her own age, big, heavy-breasted, rather plump, with a look of passion and violence about her. In fact, a formidable-looking woman, surely capable of murder. After studying her face for some minutes, Frances put her photographs, the prints and the negatives, back into the cupboard, took those of herself and the two younger women to the sitting-room, put them down on the hearth and set fire to them.

The negatives spat, blazed briefly and disappeared, making a pungent smell in the room. The prints curled at the edges and caught fire more slowly, but as she prodded them with the poker, they flared up, then smouldered into ash. Watching them, sitting on her heels, she waited until there was not a spark left, then stood up and went to the telephone.

She had a plan now, a plan of sorts. It was a gamble, but then what could she do that was not? Picking up the directory, she looked up the Sowerbys' number and dialled it.

To her satisfaction, it was a woman's voice that answered. Frances did not introduce herself.

'I've found what you were looking for,' she said softly.

There was a silence. Frances suddenly became aware of how her heart was thudding. For this was the moment when she would discover whether or not her gamble had paid off. She might have guessed totally wrongly. Mrs Sowerby might be an innocent woman who had been in bed all day with flu, feeling very ill, and if that were so, Frances would have to start thinking all over again. It seemed to her lunacy now that she had not called the police as soon as she had found Julia's body. If only she had known how simple it was going to be to find the photographs, she would have done so, and would have had plenty of time to destroy them before the police arrived. But there was not much point in thinking on those lines now. It was too late. She waited.

At last an almost whispering voice said in her ear, 'Who are you?'

She drew a shuddering breath. So she had been right. Her plan was working.

'A friend of Julia's,' she said. 'I think you'd better come here as soon as possible.'

'What do you want?' the voice asked.

'Your help,' Frances said.

'I can't come. I'm ill.'

'I think it would be advisable to make a quick recovery.'

'But I can't. My husband wouldn't hear of my going out.'

'That's your problem. I'll wait here for a little, but not for long.'

There was another silence, then the voice said, 'All right, I'll see what I can do.'

The telephone at the other end was put down. Frances put down the one that she was holding, realising that the hand that had been gripping it was clammy with sweat and had left damp marks on the instrument. She wondered if that mattered, but decided that it did not. She would have another call to make presently, which would account for the fingerprints.

She waited an hour before there came a ring at the front door bell. The early dusk of the February afternoon was already dimming the daylight. She had spent some of the time while she had had to wait stripping Julia's body of the dressing gown and night-dress that she was wearing and re-dressing it in pants and bra, jeans and sweater. It had been a terrible undertaking. In the middle of it she had felt faint and had had to go back to the sitting-room to give herself a chance to recover her self-control. But she had been afraid to wait until the other woman arrived and could help her in case the body stiffened too much to make the undressing of it possible. She knew nothing about how long it took for rigor mortis to set in. The blood-stained clothes that she removed were a problem and so was the hammer. She had not thought about that until after she had started undressing Julia, but in the end she made a bundle of them, took them out to the garage and put them into the boot of the Darnells' car. Then she went back into the house to wait.

When the ring at the door came at last and she went to answer it, she found the woman whom she had been expecting on the doorstep. Her guess about the photographs had been correct. Isobel Sowerby was a middle-aged woman, tall and thick set, with thick dark hair to her shoulders, intense dark eyes and jutting lips. She was wearing slacks and a sheepskin jacket.

Staring at Frances with deep enmity, she said, 'What am I supposed to do now?'

'We're going to arrange a suicide,' Frances answered.

'I don't understand,' the other woman said. 'If you know so much, why haven't you turned me in?'

'Because I'm involved myself. I made the mistake of not calling the police as soon as I found the body. I wanted to find some photographs of me that Oliver had and I didn't think until it was too late how difficult it was going to be to explain how I'd managed not to find Julia as soon as I got back from the church. So I'm in almost as much trouble as you are. And I think the best thing for both of us to do is to put Julia into her car and send her over the cliffs into the sea. Suicide while the balance of her mind was disturbed by the death of her husband. I couldn't arrange it alone because she's too heavy for me to carry. I had to have help.'

'All right, whatever you say,' Isobel Sowerby said. 'But give me the photographs first.'

'Afterwards,' Frances said.

'No, now, or I won't help you.'

'Afterwards,' Frances repeated.

They looked at one another with wary antagonism, then Isobel Sowerby shrugged her shoulders.

'Let's get on with it then,' she said. 'I persuaded my husband to go to the golf club to get over the funeral, and he'll stay there for a time and have a few drinks, but he'll be home presently and it won't help us to have him asking me questions.'

'How did you get into the house this morning?' Frances asked. 'I've been wondering about that.'

'The back door was unlocked, as I knew it would be. We aren't particular about locking up round here.'

'And you left in a hurry when you heard me come in.'

'Yes. Now let's get on.'

It was almost dark by then and the garage doors could not be seen from the lane outside. There was no one to see them as they carried Julia's body from the house to the car, put it in the seat beside the driver's, covered it with a rug, got into the car themselves and with Isobel Sowerby driving, since she knew the roads, started towards the coast. She drove cautiously along the twisting lanes until at last they reached the cliff-top and saw the dark chasm of the sea ahead of them.

Stopping the car close to the edge of the cliff, she and Frances got out and between them moved Julia's body into the driving seat. After that it was only a case of turning on the engine again, putting the car into low gear, slamming the doors, and standing back while it went slowly forward to the brink, seemed to teeter there for an instant, then went plunging down, the sound of the crash that it made as it hit the rocks below carrying up to them with a loudness which it seemed to Frances must carry for miles.

But afterwards there was no sign that anyone else had heard it. The darkness around them was silent. They started the long walk back.

They did not talk to one another as they walked and had reached the Darnells' cottage before Isobel Sowerby said, 'I don't know what I'm going to say to my husband. He'll have got back from the golf club long ago.'

'You'll think of something,' Frances said. She did not think that Major Sowerby would be difficult to delude. 'You could always say you've been wandering around in a state of delirium.'

'Which is what I think I've been doing,' Isobel Sowerby said. 'Now give me the photographs.'

Frances took her into the sitting-room and showed her the heap of ashes in the grate.

'I burnt them.'

Isobel Sowerby stared at them incredulously, then broke suddenly into hysterical laughter.

'What a fool I am!' she cried. 'I've always been a fool. I needn't have come at all!'

'But I needed your help, so naturally I wasn't going to tell you that,' Frances replied.

'Are those really my photographs? You really destroyed them?'

'Along with some of my own. I'd get home now as soon as I could if I were you, because I'm going to telephone the police and tell them Julia's missing.'

Still laughing, Isobel Sowerby turned and plunged out into the darkness.

Frances went to the telephone, called the police and told them that she was very concerned because she had just discovered that Mrs Darnell, who was suffering from a high fever and was in a state of shock after the death of her husband, had disappeared. Her car was missing too. Frances said that she had only just discovered this, because after the lunch that had been held in the house after the funeral, she had felt so tired that she had gone to her room to lie down and had fallen asleep and had only just woken up, gone into Mrs Darnell's room to see how she was and found it empty. She said that she knew that Mrs Darnell had been in her room at about half past one, when she had taken some food and wine up to her and Mrs Darnell had drunk a little wine but had refused the food. But at what time she had got up and gone out Frances had no idea, because she had been so sound asleep. She had heard nothing. Anything might have happened in the house without her being aware of it.

The man who answered her call said that someone would be out to see her shortly. Putting the telephone

down, Frances fetched a dustpan and brush, swept up
the ashes in the grate and flushed them down the
lavatory. Then in truth feeling as tired as she had told
the policeman that she had felt earlier, she began
to clear up the dining-room and had started on the
washing-up when the police arrived.

After that everything went surprisingly smoothly.
The police soon found the wreck of the car on the rocks
at the foot of the cliffs and the hammer and the blood-
stained nightdress and dressing-gown in the boot. They
also found fingerprints on the steering-wheel which
were later identified as Mrs Sowerby's and they found
some highly obscene photographs of her in a cupboard
in Oliver Darnell's studio. It had happened too that
Major Sowerby, in a state of great anxiety at finding his
wife missing when he returned from the golf club, had
telephoned several friends to ask if she was with them,
so without his intending it, he had destroyed any
chance that she might have had of concocting an alibi.
She told an absurd story about having been summoned
by Mrs Liley to help her get rid of the body of Julia
Darnell, whom she and not Isobel Sowerby had murdered, but the story was not believed. There was a little
doubt as to whether she could have handled the body
by herself, but she was a big, powerful woman and it
was thought that she could and she was charged with
the murder. Frances stayed on in the Darnells' cottage
until after the inquest, then when her presence was no
longer required, telephoned Mark and started for home.

As she drove, she fell into one of her rare moods of
self-examination. She was not a nice person, she
thought. Some people might even say of her that she
was rather horrible. She did not really blame Mark for
wanting to leave her and marry that little pudding of a
woman who had been infatuated with him for the last

five years. And if only he would give up his claim to the children, Frances would be quite willing to let him go. But they were the only people for whom she had ever felt any deep and lasting love. Or what she took to be love. It did not involve questioning whether it would be better for them to stay with her or with Mark, or which of their parents the girls themselves loved most. Even in her present mood of introspection, she did not ask herself that. She simply knew that they were hers, a possession from which it would be intolerable to be parted.

And horrible as perhaps she was, was she not an instrument of justice? Had she not arranged the arrest of Julia's murderess, without herself or those two foolish young women, whose photographs she had good-naturedly burnt, becoming involved? No mud would stick to any of them. None of it would splash devastatingly on to the children. Only the guilty would suffer. So why should anyone criticise her? In a state of quiet satisfaction, she drove homewards to Mark.

Without a Mark

John Gordon

John Gordon

Without a Mark

I was, I suppose, a bit young. The policeman certainly thought so.

'Mr Hughes?' he said. 'Mr Thomas Hughes?' He emphasised the mister.

'Yes,' I said.

He spread the documents out on the counter and began to read them. I tried to watch him but I was distracted by the other things going on around me. People were constantly coming into the police station through the door at my back, and I was looking around every few seconds to see if it was somebody under arrest. I saw a glint of handcuffs as one policeman lifted his coat to put his hand to his trouser pocket, and I saw a lot of people moving to and fro behind a glass screen at the other side of the counter, but there were no obvious criminals. They were in the cells, I imagined, somewhere out at the back where the dustbins would be.

The nearest thing to excitement was a man in a sheep-skin coat who, like me, produced some documents and then was told, 'The Clerk to the Court will let you know the date, sir.' He nodded – I didn't hear him say a single word all the time he was there – and left. None of it was dramatic, yet there was a feeling that these ordinary faces above the blue tunics had some kind of special knowledge; they knew of something hidden away in that building, something as terrible as an operating theatre, and you felt that they could introduce you to it and you wouldn't like it. After feeling as scared as that, it's a wonder I did what I did on the way home.

'Why isn't your father with you, son?' The policeman had dropped the mister.

'He's at work,' I said. 'He asked me to do it.'

'I see.' He kept saying 'I see' – it was about the only policeman-like thing about him. He was quite old. He looked at the documents again. 'So you are the beneficiary,' he said.

'Yes.' I knew what he meant. We'd been through it so many times with people in offices. It meant that my uncle had left everything to me.

'You are the beneficiary,' he repeated, 'not your father.'

'No,' I said. I was named after my uncle and I don't think he'd ever thought of leaving what he owned to anybody else; because there was nobody. 'He and my Dad decided it,' I said. I thought I'd better say that in case he thought there was some quarrel between them. There wasn't. My uncle was a gentle, kind man.

'I see.' The policeman looked down again at the documents. 'Well your father's signed everything, and you've signed everything, so I don't think we've got anything more to worry about.' He reached along the counter for a book with a blue back, carefully placed a piece of carbon paper between its leaves and wrote something. 'Just sign here, Thomas Hughes, and I'll give you the keys to your property.'

Your property . . . It was the first time anybody apart from my mother and father had said it, and it made me feel strange. I didn't look at the policeman but I knew he was smiling – in the distant way policemen have, as though they're looking at you through the slits of a gun turret. I think my hand trembled slightly as I took the pen.

He went to a hatch and said something to somebody inside. The keys were quickly brought out and handed over. There weren't very many – two front-door keys, one for the back door, and something that looked as though it belonged to a shed.

'You'll be glad this is all over, I suppose, Thomas Hughes,' said the policeman.

'Yes.'

'It can't have been a very nice time for you. A great shock for your Mum and Dad.'

I nodded, saying nothing. He was being kind, but I really did want to be out of that police station.

'Still, Thomas Hughes,' he said, straightening up, 'that's what inquests are for.'

'Yes,' I said, but I didn't know what he meant.

'They find out the truth.' There were only the two of us in the office and he stood looking at me, his hands spread wide apart on the counter. I felt as though I was in front of a judge. 'When two people are found like your Auntie and Uncle, somebody's got to find out what happened, isn't that so?'

He wanted me to answer so I said yes.

'They've got to find out what went wrong so it won't happen again, is that right? So other people can be warned.'

He paused, smiling at me from his gun turret, and I nodded, edging backwards.

'So that's why it's all brought out in public, Thomas Hughes. Everything. I know it's hard on your Mum and Dad, and you as well, but that's why it's done. Death by misadventure. And, as the Coroner said, a very nasty accident.' We kept our eyes on each other. He really was trying to be kind. 'So everything that can be known, is known, and you can forget about it.' He paused. 'And my advice to you is: put it all behind you. Life must go on. Good day to you, Thomas Hughes.'

I was dismissed so abruptly I think I stumbled as I turned. But then I was out in the open air, picking up my bike from where it leant against the police-station wall, and was cycling home.

The keys were still in my hand, uncomfortable against the handlebar, and I put my finger through the ring so they could dangle clear. They were the keys to my property. The fact laid hold of me again.

I was thirteen, I was riding a bike that rattled, I had 33p in my pocket and didn't think it would last out until Saturday, yet a few streets away stood a house, rooms, a garden, furniture, that all belonged to me. I stamped on the pedals and jerked forward; I couldn't help it. I wanted to weave about in the road and whirl the keys around my head.

And then, just as suddenly, I didn't want to do it at all. I wanted to go to my Uncle Tom and hand him back his keys. Sorry, I said to him. I spoke aloud, but it was a lonely road and nobody heard. I liked him; I always had. He was a thin, rather quiet man but, as I say, very gentle. Although he had the sharpest eyes I've ever seen. They laughed at you. They looked at you over the top of his spectacles, dug the funny bits out of you and laughed at them. I'd never minded because right from early on I'd done the same with him – we sort of challenged each other and enjoyed it.

He was quite old, of course; a lot older than Dad. Retired. He'd had a chemist's shop but he'd simply locked the door one day and sold up. Said he'd had enough. Typical, said my mother, who'd never quite understood him. But my father had said it must have been Alice who made him do it; made him do it simply because he liked being at the shop, meeting people.

Aunt Alice was not my father's favourite – nobody's favourite, in fact. She was tall, like my uncle, but older. She was old-fashioned, too. And sharp-tongued, especially with me. I rather liked the thought of owning the place she'd lived in – simply because she'd never have wanted it to happen. But, apart from my father, there'd been nobody else.

I was about to turn into our own road when the idea struck me. I must have had it all along, of course. You can't be given the keys of a house and told it's yours without wanting to go inside. And I'll tell you something else. It wasn't just because I liked my Uncle Tom that had made me a bit doubtful about going into the house that had been his; it was because I was a bit scared. So would anybody be about going into a house where two people had been found dead.

But I made up my mind quite suddenly and, instead of turning into our road, I went straight on and eventually turned in the other direction and rode away across the town towards the avenues. It was a fairly old part of town – the houses were much older than the one we lived in, but they were much larger – and you could tell it had been kept unchanged ever since it was built. The avenues were all named after trees and they had the proper trees planted in them as well – Beech, Oak, Sycamore. My aunt's house (as I got near it I somehow couldn't think of it as Uncle Tom's) was in Larch Avenue. And at this time in the morning there were more trees to be seen than people; in fact, as I rode into the avenue, there was nobody else in sight. No cars, just the rustle of leaves as though the trees were big feather-dusters dusting the house-fronts. I almost turned back at that thought, but then it occurred to me that this was probably the best time of all because I wouldn't have people watching me, a boy, climb the steps and unlock the front door. And the sun was shining; I don't think I could have gone in there alone at night.

So I propped my bike against the kerb and opened the wooden gate into the front garden of number fourteen. As a garden it hardly counted. It consisted of a few paving stones from between which a laurel bush grew, and a narrow grating intended to let light into the basement window below my feet. Four stone steps led up to the porch, and above that the house rose alongside its neighbours in bands of yellow and grey brick and windows that reflected back the sky like slabs of tile.

Without thinking, I had raised my hand to the knocker and just in time pulled it back. Even the slightest attempt to bring somebody from inside made my stomach shrink. But the movement of my hand had brought the key close to the lock and I knew I had at least to try it. It turned easily. The door shook slightly and then swung inwards. It was my house, but at that moment I did not want it. I hated my uncle for forcing me to be there, to be attached to it.

I began to retreat, but the key had jammed in the lock and as I came forward to free it I took a pace into the hall. It was very narrow; the whole house was very narrow, but it went through a long way to the back. The key came out of the lock, but I stood there, half in and half outside.

Coloured glass in the fanlight over the door made a pattern at the foot of the stairs. I stood watching it for a moment, collecting my thoughts. And then I looked around me.

Close to me there was an old-fashioned hatstand, quite bare of hats, but with umbrellas and walking sticks in its base, and a little drawer set below the mirror. I opened it. There were some coins inside; a small pile of silver. I expect it was money to pay the milkman or the baker, but quite suddenly I realised who could have it now; who it really belonged to. I shut the drawer quickly. It was wrong to think like that.

But the idea had been started. It burnt through me like a fuse, quickly, and I could not look at even such a dull object as the hatstand without thinking: it's mine, the drawer and the money in it, the carpet along the hall, up the stairs, branching out and bursting into all the rooms...all mine.

I put the door on the latch, and took a few steps into the hall, leaving the door open. There was nothing like ordinary fear in me, the feeling that I would hear footsteps upstairs or a whisper from the back room – whatever shreds remained of that kind of fear were silvered over with the knowledge that I was walking through my own property, that every scrap of it was mine. It was a treasure house, like being let loose in a department store at night and told you could have everything you wanted.

But I'll say this for myself, I did struggle against gloating too much, against the appearance of greed, trying to keep thoughts of my uncle in my mind, or even my aunt. She was with me particularly in the kitchen. I could see her bent over the sink, sour-faced, ready to find fault. My mother, when we were all invited to the house, which wasn't often, would offer to help in here but always came out flustered and angry, muttering that nothing she could do was right; and how, she would ask my father on the way home, how could Tom put up with her all these years?

I opened the cupboards and the door of the fridge as much in defiance of my aunt as wanting to see what was there, but everything that could have gone bad when the electricity was turned off had been taken away. I turned on the taps but nothing came from them.

I went no more then a step or two into the dining-room because it was at the back of the house and cold, and the furniture was dark and old. The curtains were drawn, and everything was stiff with my aunt's presence. I will admit that I was apprehensive in there, more than vaguely uncomfortable, and when I came into the hall I was glad of the sunshine streaming in through the open door. I stood feeling its warmth.

Really, the room I should have gone into next was the one at the front of the house. I was standing right by the door. But this was the one place that perhaps I would not enter. It was here that they had both been found, sitting in their chairs on either side of the fire-place – without a mark on them, as a neighbour, seeking to be a comfort, had told my mother. Two glasses of sherry had stood on a table between them. My uncle liked a drink. I had once, when I was much smaller, asked what made Uncle Tom smell so funny, and I think they said it was the medicine he had to make up as a chemist, but later there was no secret that he did like a drop, and he had even persuaded Aunt Alice to take a glass of sherry before a meal occasionally. This had been one of those times, because there were sherry glasses and a meal had burnt to a crisp in the kitchen. Nobody outside, however, had seen the smoke. It wasn't until next day that they had been found, still sitting by the fire, as though asleep.

I turned away from the door.

There were three storeys to the house and an attic as well as a basement, much more than I could properly explore in what was left of the morning, even if I dared. I think it was the idea of a dare that made me do what I did next – it was also like defying the constable in the police station, going behind the counter and finding out where the cells were and who was in them. I went upstairs.

Looking back, I feel it all again. A house left unoccupied for a day settles into a certain kind of stillness, a drowsiness in which the occasional hum of the refrigerator is its sleepy breathing. If it is left for a week, flies die, dishclothes dry out and become stiff, and it becomes embedded in silence. After a month the drains outside are blocked with leaves, the windows are filming over with dust, coldness is spreading like a fungus through the walls and joists, and a new kind of activity is beginning to creak and crack in every room, wearing it out with an infinite slowness. It was five weeks, and all of this had begun.

There was a grey dust mark at the edge of my finger as it ran along the banister, and on the landing there was a faintly musty smell as though dampness was fingering its way in. One door stood ajar like a sign that this place was becoming derelict. I found myself watching it, wondering if it would swing a fraction further.

Of course, it stayed still. The only light, except for that which filtered up from the hall, came from the sunlight in the room behind it. It was this that gave me the courage to go forward. I took three paces away from the stairhead and pushed it open.

It was their bedroom. The curtains, as everywhere in the house, were drawn, but they were thin and allowed a greenish light to fill up the room like water in an aquarium. I felt the chill of it. The huge, dark wardrobe was polished and glinted as though it was wet, the wallpaper had little flowers like pallid water blooms, and the counterpane of the bed hung as though washed there by the tide.

The dressing-table stood with its back to the window.

It was not the thought of valuables that drew me towards it – I knew my aunt's jewellery had been taken away for safe-keeping – but the last remnants of the dare. I simply said to myself: go across the room and come back, and then you can leave. I tried not to see myself in the mirror, moving in that empty room, and when I came to it I had my head bent, looking down.

There was a lace runner and some jars, a brush and comb, a pair of candlesticks, all neatly placed, drawn up as they would have been for my aunt's inspection. The only thing that seemed at all casual was a pair of spectacles, gold-rimmed, that lay at an angle, opened up as though put down just for a moment. I recognised them. My uncle had called them 'my apothecary glasses' for he hardly needed to use them except when making up prescriptions in the dispensary of his shop.

I picked them up. They were cold and I had to hold myself stiff to prevent a shiver, but the thin gold wires warmed so quickly in my fingers that I held them a moment longer than I had intended. They were the one thing I had seen that belonged completely to my uncle, were his alone. Quite suddenly I wanted them, not in the way I coveted the money in the drawer downstairs, but simply because they were his and he and I had liked each other.

I think I forgot where I was for a moment. The thought of him as he had been drove out all other feelings, and I was simply not aware of being alone upstairs in an empty house. I even put the glasses on. I remembered that I'd done so once before when I was very young and he had laughed. They fitted quite well. I even raised my head to do something which I had been avoiding. I looked in the mirror.

There are several kinds of shock; from outright fear to mild surprise. I think all of them came over me in a fraction of a second. To begin with there was the mild surprise of seeing how similar my face, wearing his glasses, was to Uncle Tom's; there was the shock of recognising next that I could look very much like that when I was old; and then there was the absolute fear of seeing somebody who was not myself looking at me from the mirror. I tried to tell myself that the greenish light through the curtains must have silvered my hair and aged my skin, but I was not convinced. For the face looking back at me was not mine; it was Uncle Tom's.

Yet he was dead, he and his wife with him, sitting before the fire without a mark on them.

I wanted to snatch off the glasses then, run from the room in a panic, down the stairs and out. I moved my hand. My right hand moved up an inch towards the glasses. Then stopped. I looked down. Through the glasses I could see my hand. It was distorted slightly by the lens, the fingers longer and knobbed at the knuckles. I strove to make it move, but nothing happened. And there was something more. I was dizzy because, looking down through the curved glass, I felt taller; the ground was further away.

But then I moved my feet. At least I could walk. I began to move across the bedroom, willing myself to be away from here, but although my limbs seemed longer I walked much slower. I tried to turn my head to see myself in the mirror again, hoping that a shift of angles would destroy the illusion, but my neck muscles would not obey. I was trapped inside some other body; a passenger inside some other head.

My hand touched the banister. My feet began descending the stairs. I thought I was gasping for breath, panting, yet I was aware my lungs filled and emptied steadily. I sent my mind screaming away, trying to tear myself from the mysteries of the empty house; yet the house had no mysteries. I knew every inch of it, even the nooks and crannies I had never seen.

At the foot of the stairs I could see out into the street where my bicycle stood at the kerb in the sunshine. I brought all my will into all my muscles to force myself to walk straight ahead.

Without a tremor, my head turned away from the sunshine, towards the gloomy corridor and the door of the one room I did not want to enter.

My hand went to the handle. I had the utmost fear of going in there. I pleaded with myself, whimpering within my head. My hand, almost on the handle, hesitated. I begged again, begged and begged, and gradually my hand began to draw back. I was succeeding; something had sympathy with my pleading. I panted, relaxing.

And then came the sound. The sound of somebody else in the house. Footsteps and a voice, harsh, high-pitched, scolding. I was aware of hatred for it; detestation of the skinny female face it came from. There was a burst of hatred in my head, so violent that for a moment it obliterated me. I did not exist inside my own head. And my hand was on the handle and I was inside the room.

Nothing had changed. I crouched within my head as my limbs moved deliberately, carrying me across the carpet. The curtains were thicker in here and the light was dimmer, but I had no difficulty in avoiding the furniture. I knew precisely where everything should be. I closed the door behind me and heard the heavy door curtain swing on its rail, cutting out sound from outside. And air.

I saw the table. I lingered by it. I knew what I was looking for. I knew much more than I could possibly have known. It was the sherry glasses I was seeking – the sherry glasses that had stood there, both full, untouched next morning. For it was the gas fire that had killed them as they sat, facing each other, hating each other, before they'd had a chance to drink their sherry and have their meal. The fumes from the blocked flue had crept into the room as they sat, making them drowsy, making their heads nod, letting them breathe until the poison stopped them breathing altogether. They had died without a mark on them.

But the sherry glasses. The sherry glasses filled my mind. I could see them as they had stood, the amber liquid glowing in the red light from the fire. But they had gone. Somebody had taken them away and emptied them. For a moment I felt relief, but suddenly my heart – the heart which, like my limbs, did not belong to me – began to beat wildly, almost choking me.

I was filled with the sickening fear, a nightmare in which I had committed the most terrible kind of deed and could not flee from it or undo what I had done.

I found myself stumbling towards where the sideboard bulged massively against the wall. I was in such haste I almost fell against it, and then I was reaching down, opening the doors. There were bottles there, and glasses. On my knees, I reached inside, pushing bottles to one side, hearing them clink and fall over, and then, at the very back and out of sight, I felt the one I wanted, cold in my fingers.

I brought the bottle out. I knew it was sherry even though the label was turned away from me. The special bottle. Her bottle. I crouched as I twisted it in my hands. I was checking that there was no mistake. I knew what to look for and my own finger pointed out to me what made it different. I saw my old, yellowed nail point at the tiny ink cross made in the corner.

In the kitchen the taps had gone dry but I knew where to turn them on under the draining board. I heard the water rattle in the pipes and then spit, brown with rust, into the sink. It was only then that I began pouring the golden liquid from the bottle. I watched it swirl round in the whiteness of the sink, drawn all the time to the black hole that swallowed it. And as it went, I felt the tension going out of my muscles. The poison that had been meant for her had vanished.

I tried to lift my head, expecting to be denied, but this time the muscles obeyed me. There was a little kitchen mirror just to one side of the sink. I caught a glimpse of myself and turned towards it. My uncle's face looked back at me. And then the spectacles slid from my nose and smashed at my feet.

I stooped to pick them up.

When I straightened I could no longer see his face in the mirror. I was looking at myself – except that when I smiled, full of relief, the smile on my lips was more his than mine. And the relief was his, too. The fumes had prevented his crime, and now the bottle would never be able to harm anyone.

Dear George

Cathy Ace

Cathy Ace

Dear George

January 1st

So here it is, the first day of the year I kill George. This diary will be a record of all that I do this year, so that one day everyone will know how clever I was. I'll tell you, dear diary, everything. No one else will know our plans – but after ten years of gradually hating dear, sweet George more and more, day after day, month after month, I'm going to do something about it. I'm going to stop him snoring; stop his armpits smelling; stop him scraping his knife on his plate; stop him eyeing up young girls; stop his palms sweating; stop him picking his nose – stop him dead.

I'm going to keep you hidden underneath my one and only frilly nightie. George never looks in the wardrobe drawer where I keep it hidden. So no one will know that you're there except you and me. And we won't be telling, will we?

January 28th

I think I'm doing very well to find the time to tell you all about what's been going on – every day. I find the time because you're very special to me. You understand me – not like him! He's out at the pub again with his 'mates'! I expect they'll all be sitting there cracking dirty jokes, and he'll be busy chatting up that new barmaid. I saw her in town the other week. Little tart! All boobs and no brain, that's what I say. Mind you, I feel better knowing that I'll be at dear George's funeral in July. Oh, I'm sorry, didn't I tell you? I decided yesterday that I'd kill him on July 4th. It's Independence Day in America you know. Good that, eh? The day I get rid of George will be celebrated right at the other side of the world. Clever.

February 1st

I've been thinking. I don't know how we'll manage when George is dead. I haven't got any money, and I've never had a job. I don't think I could do anything. Except horrible things like working in a shop, or a factory, and I really don't want to do that. I don't know how to get round this one at all. George hasn't got any money. Our savings in the Post Office wouldn't go very far. What shall I do? Oh, yes, that's a good idea. Get George to insure his life, then I get the money when he's dead. You're very clever, aren't you? Almost as clever as me!

February 4th

I'm going to talk to George about life insurance tonight. When he comes to bed I'm going to talk to him about it – all casual like. We agreed £100,000 didn't we? Yes, I know you think that's greedy, but I'll want to live it up a bit when boring old George has gone. I'll tell you tomorrow how it goes. I've got to have a bath now. It's Wednesday; we always do it on a Wednesday, unless George doesn't feel like it. Knowing my luck he will tonight.

February 5th

I had to tell George that I wanted us both to insure ourselves, so as not to make him suspicious, but he says we can't afford it anyway.

I don't believe him. I'm going to get the man from the Pru to come and talk to us; he goes to Iris and David's every month to get his money. Iris is going to ask him to call here next time. Iris said I look tired today. That's because George came in late last night and woke me up. He never smells of drink, but I know he's been drinking. He says he's at the Country and Western Club, but that's just an excuse to go out boozing where he knows I won't follow. Maybe next Wednesday I'll go along with him, see what he really gets up to. That would finish him! That would blow his little cover story for late nights out!

February 12th

Sorry I didn't talk to you last night: I got all dressed up, and when George came in from the office I told him I was going out with him. That shocked him! And you'll never guess what we did – we *did* go to the blessed Country and Western Club! Lots of people said hello to him as we went in, lots of women, that is. But he didn't drink at all – only orange juice. He did that to make me think that he never ever drinks, but I know different. Anyway, even though he didn't drink, we still did it when we came home. Honestly, you sit in a corner not talking to anyone, have to listen to that awful racket all night, and still have to come home and do it – terrible! I don't think I'll bother again!

February 27th

We both signed the insurance papers today! The fool! He didn't have a clue! Now when I kill him I'll be rich too! I can hardly wait. The 4th July seems a very long time away. Perhaps I should reconsider that date. As soon as he's out of the way I can go on a lovely cruise: people would expect me to get away for a while after all the fuss and police and all that. I suppose there will be a fuss. What do you think? Yes, I think so too. But it's the only way to do it – shoot George then give myself up to the police and tell them it was An Accident. Besides, I want to see his face as I pull the trigger – see his stupid eyes show the realisation of what I'm doing to him: see him getting the point for once in his stupid, miserable life.

It's all his fault anyway, for keeping the gun. If I hadn't seen it in his desk last year I'd never have got this brilliant idea. It's probably illegal to have the gun here: but *that's* all right with dear George because it was his high and mighty father's! I'm going to take it onto the Common next week to check that it works; there are only three bullets in it but I need to use one just to make sure I know how to make it shoot properly. I'll take the car on Saturday and wait until there's no one around – so long as I don't point it at anything except the ground it can't do any harm. Anyway, goodnight now. I'm sorry I haven't been writing in you as tidily as usual today, but that copperplate is very hard to keep going, and my hands are sore from wringing out the bedroom curtains this afternoon. Still, the washing-machine man will be here tomorrow and then the spinner will be working again.

March 7th

I shot the gun today! I didn't realise it would make such a noise! It frightened me to death! (What a funny thing to say – it won't frighten George to death, it'll shoot George to death!) No one heard me though; it was far too cold for anyone to be out on the Common. I hurt my wrist, too; I held the gun in two hands like they do on the telly, but it still pushed back a lot. At least I know I can do it.

And dear George didn't suspect anything, of course. I asked if I could borrow the car to go to Legge's, over near Madge's and I put the gun in the bottom of my blue shopping bag wrapped in an old carrier bag. He just sat there glued to the bloody football and threw the keys at me. I nearly laughed – if only he'd guessed! Him and his beloved West Ham – well, it's the last season I'll have to put up with *Match of the Day*. Come to think of it, I wouldn't mind shooting Jimmy Hill too!

March 12th
Did the washing today. One thing I really hate is the way George refuses to use Kleenex, and will insist on using real hankies. I'm the one who's got to wash them! They're revolting! But he won't listen to me. I'd make him wash them himself, but he wouldn't get them clean, and I'm certainly not having her next door seeing dirty washing on the line. I was doing the ironing when I tried to work out how many of George's shirts I've ironed since we've been married – it's about four thousand. Probably more. I feel as though I've done them all today! I'm getting tired more quickly these days. Getting headaches too. George isn't at all sympathetic. He says I should get my eyes seen to. He'll find out if there's anything wrong with my eyes when I hit him with that little bullet!

April 27th
Our Wedding Anniversary! What a bundle of laughs today was, dear diary. I gave George a card and a new pair of grey woollen socks from Marks and Spencers. He gave me a box of chocolates – then he ate all the soft ones! Pig! I hate him! Do you know he actually laughed at me as he ate the coffee cream! That was *it*. Dear, dear diary, I know we agreed that we'd wait, but I *can't*

wait any longer. He's a pig. He hates me as much as I hate him, I'm sure of that, he wouldn't have eaten all the soft ones if he didn't would he?

Eleven years ago today I promised to love, honour and obey him. Well today I'm promising to love, honour and obey myself. Please don't be upset. I'll keep you in the picture. I'm going to do it this Saturday. Then there'll just be you and me, and the money too, of course!

May 2nd

I know I'm early, but I had to talk to you – I'm so excited! I've smashed the glass in the back door, inwards like we agreed, and I've put my big shopping bag in the middle of the living room and filled it with all our bits of silver. It's already dark, but the gun is safe in my dressing-gown pocket. I'll tell the police I was in bed with a headache when I heard the noise, picked up the gun and went downstairs. I'll tell them how terrified I was, and when I saw a shadowy figure at the door coming towards me, that I thought it was a burglar, or a rapist, and shot at it. Then I'll tell them how I discovered it was dear George. They'll see how upset I am and I'll get away with it! Then it will be just the three of us. You, me and the money. It won't be long now. He never puts the light on when he comes in. I'll put you away now. We may not be able to talk for some time.

*

The foreman of the jury rose from his seat.

'Not guilty.'

Clear and loud NOT GUILTY! It was An Accident – a dreadful, tragic Accident. The past few days had been a tremendous strain: the newspapers had picked up the story, and photographs of 'The Victim' and 'The

Accused' had appeared everywhere. But now it was over, the jury agreed with the general public – tragic, but certainly not premeditated. The judge was saying something, then there were lots of congratulations being shouted from the gallery. Outside were more photographers, and, thankfully, a taxi. Not back to the house – not that porch where it had happened. No, to a hotel room: a bright, impersonal room with just a hint of luxury. Oh yes, that insurance money would come in very handy!

*

George Melrose turned on the television set, then bounced on the edge of the hotel bed. The afternoon film crackled in monochrome – there was Katherine Hepburn in a dressing gown, just like Joyce when she had come downstairs that night. George had looked at her disapproving eyes peering from underneath her curlers for the last time, walked towards her, took her hands, pointed the gun towards her heart and pulled the trigger. The blood had ruined the dressing gown of course. Then he had put the gun in Joyce's hand and shot again, this time breaking the glass in the big oak hallstand.

The police hadn't believed George that Joyce had been trying to kill him. He had never thought they would. After all, George was such an inoffensive chap, why should Joyce want to kill him? Unless she had a screw loose, of course. No, George was quiet, a tee-totaller who was hard-working, and happy to stay at home watching the box. No one had known him to go out except to his Country and Western Club, where he was a respected and diligent Club Secretary – they'd all come to the court to say so!

The police hadn't known what to believe, until they found the diary. It really had been very clever of him to hide it under her nightie: for months it had been hidden in the glove compartment of the car, in a plastic bag to keep it clean. George had carefully filled in each day's entry in painstakingly formed copperplate, just as in the calligraphy book now also to be found in Joyce's wardrobe.

George rang room service and ordered a cream tea. The weather was brightening, perhaps the blossom would liven itself up a bit now, thought George. Joyce had liked the blossom: it made her sneeze though, of course! Miserable, boring, plain, stupid Joyce. It really was incredible that everyone now believed she could have been bright enough to think up what was, after all, a very clever plan! People were so stupid!

*

Inspector Glover and his wife were having a late supper. They rarely discussed work, but the Melrose case had aroused much interest nationwide, and Glover's name had become known as a result. Betty Glover collected the dirty plates from the table and pushed them into the soapy water in the sink.

'You look tired, Evan.'

'It's been a hard day. I won't be sorry to get off to bed.'

'Look, Evan, I know we don't usually talk about things, but if you want to chat about this one – you go ahead.'

Evan Glover finished his tea and carefully placed the cup in the centre of the recess in the saucer.

'Don't worry, love, a good night's sleep will cure me. I just haven't felt right about this Melrose case all along – there's something we've missed, but not something you can put your finger on. And no matter how much of a gut feeling I've got, you can't convict a man on the basis of my indigestion. Anyway, he's cleared. That diary did it – all the experts agreed it was the work of someone with a few marbles loose. Almost childlike. Still, it made it perfectly clear she intended to do him in. Even covered the double insurance angle. Nice chap, you know. Quiet, almost invisible, quite colourless. Yes, that's it, colourless.'

Betty Glover wiped her hands on the tea towel, then spread the dishcloth over the taps to dry.

'Put some water in that cup before you come up, Evan. I'm going to make a move now. Don't you be too long.'

'Night, love,' called Evan to the receding figure.

'Mind you,' called back his wife, 'if I was going to kill you and give myself up straight away I'd never put my hair in curlers. Everyone looks awful in curlers. She must have been mad!'

Evan Glover was stunned. He stared open-mouthed at the china cabinet as though it had uttered the words itself...

The Lieabout

Margery Allingham

Margery Allingham

The Lieabout

I still have the brooch but I can hardly wear it. I thought of throwing it away once, but it is so very pretty. I don't think it is valuable but I have never dared to take it into a jeweller's to find out. It is a very awkward position.

I might have sent it back to the people who owned it, in fact I ought to have done that, but if ever it was traced to me who would believe my story?

It was when we lived in London. We had a small flat in a courtyard leading off High Holborn, right in the city. The courtyard was really only the foot of an air-shaft striking down amid enormous office buildings. There were only two doors in it; one belonged to a printing works and the other one was ours.

When you opened our door you found yourself at the foot of a flight of steep stairs, at the top of which were our three rooms and a sort of corridor called a kitchenette-bath.

Our domain had once been the caretaker's premises of the insurance building which was below us and still ran right through to the main street. By the time we went there it had been converted into two shops. These shops were empty when we arrived and remained so for nearly a year, although from time to time gangs of workmen were very busy in them, obliterating, we supposed, still more of the atmosphere of insurance.

There are several odd things about living in the city.

One is the quiet of the place at night. When we moved to the country the noises of the night birds were almost too much for us after that deathly peace of the City of London when the offices have closed.

Another curious thing is the surprising intimacy and friendliness of it all. In no village in which I ever lived did I acquire so many acquaintances.

The shops where one could buy the ordinary necessities of life as opposed to an adding machine, a battleship or a two-thousand-guinea emerald ring were all of the small and homely variety and were nearly all of them tucked away in courtyards like our own. The people who owned them were friendly and obliging and told us their family histories at the slightest encouragement.

The news-sellers and the hawkers were other regulars who were anxious to gossip or pass the time of day, and as I walked down the crowded pavement with my shopping basket on my arm I found I had as many people to nod to as if I were in a small town street which had suddenly become overrun with half a million foreigners.

I first met the Lieabout in our own yard. He was sitting there one evening among a pile of packing-cases from the printing works when I went out to play with Addlepate. Addlepate leapt on him, mistaking him for a sack of waste paper in which he delighted. The misapprehension led to a sort of introduction and after a while the Lieabout watched the dog to see that he did not go out into the traffic and commit suicide and I went up to get the man some tea.

He was a frail old person with a beaky face and little bright red eyes like a ferret or one of the old black rats who come out and dance on the cobbles in the small hours.

All lieabouts are necessarily dirty. Genuine tramping can never be a hygienic method of life. But he was horribly so. He looked as though he had just slipped down from his niche among the gargoyles of St Paul's before the cleaners could get him. He was sooty with London, and his garments, which were varied and of dubious origin, were all the same grey-black colour, and not with dye.

He was glad of the tea, and when I said I had not seen him about before, he explained that he had come up from Cheapside, where he had been spending the summer. He did not ask for money and I did not offer him any, naturally. We parted friends, he to return to his packing-cases in which he was making himself a temporary home and I to my work upstairs.

He lived in the packing-cases for nearly a week and we kept up a nodding acquaintance.

I was out shopping one morning when I saw the brooch. It was on a lower shelf in the window of one of those very big jewellers and silversmiths whose principal trade seems to be in challenge cups and presentation plate. The shop was not quite opposite the entrance to our courtyard but about fifty yards down on the other side of the traffic. I stood for some time looking at the brooch. It consisted of seven large topaz set in oxydised silver and the finished effect was rather like the rose window in Notre Dame.

I was still gazing at it when the Lieabout appeared at my elbow.

'Nice, ain't it?' he said. 'Goin' to 'ave it?'

I laughed and indicated my basket, which held one of Addlepate's Friday bones protruding rather disgustingly from a sea of lettuce.

'Not this week. Food's gone up,' I said, and would have passed on, but the ornament had evidently attracted him, too, for he came nearer to look at it and I should have had to brush past him to get into the jostling stream in the middle of the pavement again.

'It's not worfa thousand quid,' he observed, after a moment or so of contemplation. 'Go in an' arsk 'em. They'll say a tenner, I betcha.'

'Very likely,' I said. 'And what should I do?'

He grinned at me, disclosing a most disreputable assortment of different-size teeth.

'Same as me, I reckon,' he said. 'Beat it like one o'clock. 'Day, lady.'

I went home and forgot all about the incident and the next day was Saturday.

Up to this point the story was quite ordinary, but once the police came into it the whole thing became a little fantastic.

Saturday morning in the city always has a last day at boarding school atmosphere. Fewer strangers swoop out of the fat red buses or come boiling up out of the tubes, and those that do appear are definitely in holiday mood. When the big clock of St Paul's strikes noon the exodus begins, and by a quarter to one the streets look like a theatre after the show is over.

The road outside our courtyard, which all the week had been a sort of nightmare Brooklands, turned suddenly into a great river of dull glass, with only an occasional bus or taxi speeding happily down its wide expanse.

There were people about, of course, but only a dozen or so, and the city policemen in their enormous helmets, which they use as small personal suitcases, I believe, stood out, lonely and important.

It was nearly two o'clock on this particular Saturday afternoon when the police arrived. My husband leant out of the studio window and reported that there were two large bobbies on the step. I went down to open the door. None of our visitors had left a car outside the yard gates for some considerable time, but although my conscience was clear, much clearer than it is now, I felt vaguely uneasy. One policeman may be a friend, but two are the Law.

On the step I found two of the largest, bluest specimens I have ever seen and they were both vastly uncomfortable. They hesitated, eyeing first me and then each other with embarrassment.

I waited awkwardly for them to begin, and presently the larger one spoke.

'I wonder if you'd do me a personal favour, Ma'am?' he said.

It was such an unexpected request that I gaped at him, and he continued:

'I want you to go out into the street and look in the empty shop next door. Don't say nothing to anyone. Just behave perfectly casual, and then come back and tell us what you think you see.'

I began to feel a trifle lightheaded, but they were certainly real policemen and, anyway, Addlepate was barking his head off at the top of the stairs.

'All right,' I said stupidly. 'Aren't you coming?'

The other constable shook his head.

'No, Ma'am. We don't want a crowd to collect. That's our idea. See?'

I went off obediently, and as soon as I turned out of the yard I saw that any hopes my official friends might have cherished concerning the absence of a crowd were doomed to disappointment. Everyone in the street seemed to be converging on the first of the empty shops, and I saw another policeman hurrying down the road towards the excitement.

On the step of the shop stood my friend the Lieabout. He was making a tremendous noise.

'It's a disgrice!' he was shouting. 'A bloomin' disgrice! It's bin there five days to my knowledge. Look at it. Look at it!'

I peered in through the plate glass and suddenly saw what he meant. The sight made me feel slightly sick. At the back of the shop was an archway leading into a further salon, which was lit by a skylight. All kinds of decorators' debris was strewn around, but among the whitewash pails, the planks and the trestles, was something covered with an old coat and a lump of sacking. The shape was suggestive. But the thing that made it horrible was the boot. The boot stuck out from beneath the coat so naturally and yet so lifelessly.

'It's a corp!' shrieked the Lieabout, to the crowd which had just reached us. 'A corp! Bin there five days. The p'lice won't do nothink. It's a murder, that's wot it is. A murdered corp!'

He turned to me.

'What you waitin' for lady? Go and tell the rozzers it's a corp.'

His voice in my ear recalled me to my senses and I hurried back to my visitors. They were polite but impatient when I gave them my opinion, and it suddenly dawned upon me why I had been singled out for their confidence. A police officer is not allowed to enter private property without authority, nor do the regulations let him ask the owners of such property for permission to enter. But once he is invited in, and has a witness to prove it, he can go wherever his good sense tells him his duty lies.

'If you get out of our bedroom window on to the roof at the back of the shop you could look through the skylight,' I said. 'Would you care to?'

They were upstairs in an instant, and I had barely time to explain to my astonished husband before they were in the bedroom, negotiating the window. I say 'negotiating' because their climb through it required finesse, and a delicacy one would hardly have expected in men of their bulk.

It was one of those awkward old-fashioned sliding casements which permit a space about two and a half feet by one and a quarter when opened to their fullest extent.

It took a little time but out they went at last, helmets and all, and my husband with them. They disappeared over the roofs, and I was left to await their return.

However, by this time an entirely unsuspected blood-lust had taken possession of me and, unable to control my impatience where I was, I trotted down into the yard again and out into the street.

To be honest, I did not reach the street. The crowd was packed solid across our entrance, all straining and jostling to peer into the window of the shop next door.

I climbed up on the iron gate which closed the yard at night, and saw over the people's heads a great expanse of empty street to the east, while the west was packed with every vehicle which had passed that way since the Lieabout's sensational find.

It was because I was prevented by the angle of the wall from seeing my two police friends descending into the shop through the skylight that I was an exception from the rest of the crowd, and did not have my attention diverted from the excitement over the way.

I saw the long black car pull up outside the jeweller's shop and I saw the three men spring out of it. It was not until the crash of broken glass reached me, as the brick went through the window, that I realised that anything untoward was afoot.

The rest happened so quickly that I hardly followed it. I had a confused impression of flying figures, something flashing in the autumn sun and then of the black car sliding round like a speedboat in the broad road and flying away with smooth acceleration. In a moment it had gone completely. I could not even see which way it turned at the end of the street. Nothing but the ragged hole in the window, with a scared assistant's face peering through it, remained to show that the raid had occurred.

At that moment the first policeman to get down into the empty shop must have pulled away the coat, revealed the neatly arranged sacks and distemper tins beneath, and kicked the old boot away angrily, for the crowd suddenly became aware of the other sensation, and surged off across the road to gape anew.

It was extraordinarily neat. The whole thing had been done in one of the most important streets without anyone being able to give a clear picture of any of the men involved.

We heard all about the robbery from the tobacconist on the corner.

Ten thousand pounds' worth of valuables had been snatched, he said, including the gold state salt-cellar which an ancient and worshipful company was presenting to a foreign royal bridegroom, and which had been on view there for a few privileged days. A little small stuff went, too, he said; a couple of trays of rings and several oddments.

I never saw the Lieabout again. Foolishly I supposed that, after making such an ass of himself by his false alarm, he did not care to show his face in the neighbourhood and had moved off to another corner of the town.

The parcel came a week later. I found it in the letter box one night when we came in from a show.

It was the topaz brooch. It lay upon a mat of cottonwool, and there was a note with it written in a neat, educated hand. The message was brief and only too enlightening.

'Very many thanks for your valuable assistance,' it ran. 'Congratulate you. Very gratefully yours.'

There was no signature and the package had not been through the post.

So you see the problem: What should Mrs A. do now?

The Wrong Category

Ruth Rendell

Ruth Rendell

The Wrong Category

There hadn't been a killing now for a week. The evening paper's front page was devoted instead to the economic situation and an earthquake in Turkey. But page three kept up the interest in this series of murders. On it were photographs of the six victims all recognisably belonging to the same type. There, in every case although details of feature naturally varied, were the same large liquid eyes, full soft mouth, and long dark hair.

Barry's mother looked up from the paper. 'I don't like you going out at night.'

'What, me?' said Barry.

'Yes, you. All these murders happened round here. I don't like you going out after dark. It's not as if you had to, it's not as if it was for work.' She got up and began to clear the table but continued to speak in a low whining tone. 'I wouldn't say a word if you were a big chap. If you were the size of your cousin Ronnie I wouldn't say a word. A fellow your size doesn't stand a chance against that maniac.'

'I see,' said Barry. 'And whose fault is it I'm only five feet two? I might just point out that a woman of five feet that marries a bloke only two inches more can't expect to have giants for kids. Right?'

'I sometimes think you only go roving about at night, doing what you want, to prove you're as big a man as your cousin Ronnie.'

Barry thrust his face close up to hers. 'Look, leave off, will you?' He waved the paper at her. 'I may not have the height but I'm not in the right category. Has that occurred to you? Has it?'

'All right, all right. I wish you wouldn't be always shouting.'

In his bedroom Barry put on his new velvet jacket and dabbed cologne on his wrists and neck. He looked spruce and dapper. His mother gave him an apprehensive glance as he passed her on his way to the back door, and returned to her contemplation of the pictures in the newspaper. Six of them in two months. The girlish faces, doe-eyed, diffident, looked back at her or looked aside or stared at distant unknown objects. After a while she folded the paper and switched on the television. Barry, after all, was not in the right category, and that must be her comfort.

He liked to go and look at the places where the bodies of the victims had been found. It brought him a thrill of danger and a sense of satisfaction. The first of them had been strangled very near his home on a path which first passed between draggled allotments, then became an alley plunging between the high brown wall of a convent and the lower red brick wall of a school.

Barry took this route to the livelier part of the town, walking rapidly but without fear and pausing at the point – a puddle of darkness between lamps – where the one they called Pat Leston had died. It seemed to him, as he stood there, that the very atmosphere, damp, dismal, and silent, breathed evil and the horror of the act. He appreciated it, inhaled it, and then passed on to seek, on the waste ground, the common, in a deserted back street of condemned houses, those other murder scenes. After the last killing they had closed the underpass, and Barry found to his disappointment that it was still closed.

He had walked a couple of miles and had hardly seen a soul. People stayed at home. There was even some kind of panic, he had noticed, when it got to six and the light was fading and the buses and tube trains were emptying themselves of the last commuters. In pairs they scurried. They left the town as depopulated as if a plague had scoured it.

Entering the high street, walking its length, Barry saw no one, apart from those protected by the metal and glass of motor vehicles, but an old woman hunched on a step. Bundled in dirty clothes, a scarf over her head and a bottle in her hand, she was as safe as he – as far, or farther, from the right category.

But he was still on the watch. Next to viewing the spots where the six had died, he best enjoyed singling out the next victim. No one, for all the boasts of the newspapers and the policemen, knew the type as well as he did. Slight and small-boned, long-legged, sway-backed, with huge eyes, pointed features, and long dark hair. He was almost sure he had selected the Italian one as a potential victim some two weeks before the event, though he could never be certain.

So far today he had seen no one likely, in spite of watching with fascination the exit from the tube on his own way home. But now, as he entered the Red Lion and approached the bar, his eye fell on a candidate who corresponded to the type more completely than anyone he had yet singled out. Excitement stirred in him. But it was unwise, with everyone so alert and nervous, to be caught staring. The barman's eyes were on him. He asked for a half of lager, paid for it, tasted it, and, as the barman returned to rinsing glasses, turned slowly to appreciate to the full that slenderness, that soulful timid look, those big expressive eyes, and that mane of black hair.

But things had changed during the few seconds his back had been turned. Previously he hadn't noticed that there were two people in the room, another as well as the candidate, and now they were sitting together. From intuition, at which Barry fancied himself as adept, he was sure the girl had picked the man up. There was something in the way she spoke as she lifted her full glass which convinced him, something in her look, shy yet provocative.

He heard her say, 'Well, thank you, but I didn't mean to...' and her voice trailed away, drowned by the other's brashness.

'Catch my eye? Think nothing of it, love. My pleasure. Your fella one of the unpunctual sort, is he?'

She made no reply. Barry was fascinated, compelled to stare, by the resemblance to Pat Leston, by more than that, by seeing in this face what seemed a quintessence, a gathering together and a concentrating here of every quality variously apparent in each of the six. And what gave it a particular piquancy was to see it side by side with such brutal ugliness. He wondered at the girl's nerve, her daring to make overtures. And now she was making them afresh, actually laying a hand on his sleeve.

'I suppose you've got a date yourself?' she said.

The man laughed. 'Afraid I have, love. I was just whiling away ten minutes.' He started to get up.

'Let me buy you a drink.'

His answer was only another harsh laugh. Without looking at the girl again, he walked away and through the swing doors out into the street. That people could expose themselves to such danger in the present climate of feeling intrigued Barry, his eyes now on the girl who was also leaving the pub. In a few seconds it was deserted, the only clients likely to visit it during that evening all gone.

A strange idea, with all its amazing possibilities, crossed his mind and he stood on the pavement, gazing the length of the High Street. But the girl had crossed the road and was waiting at the bus stop, while the man was only just visible in the distance, turning into the entrance of the underground car park.

Barry banished his idea, ridiculous perhaps and, to him, rather upsetting, and he crossed the road behind the oncoming bus, wondering how to pass the rest of the evening. Review once more those murder scenes, was all that suggested itself to him and then go home.

It must have been the wrong bus for her. She was still waiting. And as Barry approached, she spoke to him, 'I saw you in the pub.'

'Yes,' he said. He never knew how to talk to girls. They intimidated and irritated him, especially when they were taller than he, and most of them were. The little thin ones he despised.

'I thought,' she said hesitantly, 'I thought I was going to have someone to see me home.'

Barry made no reply. She came out of the bus shelter, quite close to him, and he saw that she was much bigger and taller than he had thought at first.

'I must have just missed my bus. There won't be another for ten minutes.' She looked, and then he looked, at the shiny desert of this shopping centre, lighted and glittering and empty, pitted with the dark holes of doorways and passages. 'If you're going my way,' she said, 'I thought maybe...'

'I'm going through the path,' he said. Round there that was what everyone called it, the path.

'That'll do me.' She sounded eager and pleading. 'It's

a short cut to my place. Is it all right if I walk along with you?'

'Suit yourself,' he said. 'One of them got killed down there. Doesn't that bother you?'

She only shrugged. They began to walk along together up the yellow and white glazed street, not talking, at least a yard apart. It was a chilly damp night, and a gust of wind caught them as, past the shops, they entered the path. The wind blew out the long red silk scarf she wore and she tucked it back inside her coat. Barry never wore a scarf, though most people did at this time of the year. It amused him to notice just how many did, as if they had never taken in the fact that all those six had been strangled with their own scarves.

There were lamps in this part of the path, attached by iron brackets to the red wall and the brown. Her sharp-featured face looked greenish in the light, and gaunt and scared. Suddenly he wasn't intimidated by her any more or afraid to talk to her.

'Most people,' he said, 'wouldn't walk down here at night for a million pounds.'

'You do,' she said. 'You were coming down here alone.'

'And no one gave me a million,' he said cockily. 'Look, that's where the first one died, just round this corner.'

She glanced at the spot expressionlessly and walked on ahead of Barry. He caught up with her. If she hadn't been wearing high heels she wouldn't have been that much taller than he. He pulled himself up to his full height, stretching his spine, as if effort and desire could make him as tall as his cousin Ronnie.

'I'm stronger than I look,' he said. 'A man's always stronger than a woman. It's the muscles.'

He might not have spoken for all the notice she took.

The walls ended and gave place to low railings behind which the allotments, scrubby plots of cabbage stumps and waterlogged weeds, stretched away. Beyond them, but a long way off, rose the backs of tall houses hung with wooden balconies and iron staircases. A pale moon had come out and cast over this dismal prospect a thin cold radiance.

'There'll be someone killed here next,' he said. 'It's just the place. No one to see. The killer could get away over the allotments.'

She stopped and faced him. 'Don't you ever think about anything but those murders?'

'Crime interests me. I'd like to know why he does it.' He spoke insinuatingly, his resentment of her driven away by the attention she was at last giving him. 'Why d'you think he does it? It's not for money or sex. What's he got against them?'

'Maybe he hates them.' Her own words seemed to frighten her and, strangely, she pulled off the scarf which the wind had again been flapping, and thrust it into her coat pocket. 'I can understand that.' She looked at him with a mixture of dislike and fear. 'I hate men, so I can understand it,' she said, her voice trembling and shrill. 'Come on, let's walk.'

'No.' Barry put out his hand and touched her arm. His fingers clutched her coat sleeve. 'No, you can't just leave it there. If he hates them, why does he?'

'Perhaps he's been turned down too often,' she said, backing away from him. 'Perhaps a long time ago one of them hurt him. He doesn't want to kill them but he can't help himself.' As she flung his hand off her arm the words came spitting out. 'Or he's just ugly. Or little, like you.'

Barry stood on tip-toe to bring himself to her height. He took a step towards her, his fists up. She backed against the railings and a long shudder went through her. Then she wheeled away and began to run, stumbling because her heels were high. It was those heels or the roughness of the ground or the new darkness as clouds dimmed the moon that brought her down.

Collapsed in a heap, one shoe kicked off, she slowly raised her head and looked up into Barry's eyes. He made no attempt to touch her. She struggled to her feet, wiped her grazed and bleeding hands on the scarf and immediately, without a word, they were locked together in the dark.

Several remarkable features distinguished this murder from the others. There was blood on the victim who had fair hair instead of dark, though otherwise strongly resembling Patrick Leston and Dino Facci. Apparently, since Barry Halford had worn no scarf the murderer's own had been used. But ultimately it was the evidence of a slim dark-haired customer of the Red Lion which led the police to the conclusion that the killer of these seven young men was a woman.

Millie Murray

A Blessing in Disguise

Out of every tragedy must come some good. Is so mi granny always tell me when something bad happen: 'Wilima, don't worry yurself, in a lickle time you will see a blessing come out of dis situation.' Every time mi think of mi granny, mi think of mi niece Celeste. Mi remember telling her de same thing when her husband died and her friend Florica turn mad: 'Celeste, even though de situation is bad, a blessing is soon to come,' and yu know it was true!

When mi sister Lilith went back to Jamaica fi live out de rest fi her days, Celeste came fi live with me. She was training fi be dancer. Every day she would exercise before she went fi college and after she had spent all day dere, she would still come home and practise.

'Celeste, yu will wear yurself out, chile?'

She would say between breaths, 'No I won't, Auntie, practice makes perfect.'

What could mi say to dat?

We were very happy living together, mi and Celeste. She hardly made any mess, she never did go out to disco and mi never hear her talk bout any bwoyfriend. Mi was glad in a way, because mi know how man can stop a woman from looking out fi herself. Hmm, is so dem call love.

Mi did have fi give up mi cooking job because fi mi age,

it nearly bruck mi heart, so all mi could do was cook at home. Celeste did love mi cooking but every minute she a 'check her diet'! Hmm. On Sundays mi love fi cook up a big big dinner: rice and peas, chicken or beef and some curry goat, some sweet potato roast up tender, corn and green beans, and even Irish baked potato. Yes mi dear, all dat fi one meal. Den bout a hour after mi would bring out some Gizadas with thick thick coconut pon de top and each piece mi bite come in like a slice of heaven. Then mi have to loosen mi skirt band til most of de time mi start fi wear mi broad-cut summer frock.

'Auntie, you shouldn't eat so much, it's not good for your heart!'

Mi just smile, she was so concern fi mi! 'Dat's all right dear, God looks after his own.' All Celeste do is nibble!

De only person Celeste had as a visitor was Florica. She call her her friend. Mi wasn't so sure. She had some long long fingernail that come in like claw. Mi granny always sey, 'Wilima, any ooman dat have long long fingernail, nar trust dem, especially with yur man!'

Celeste was kindness itself. Just looking at her, with her fine bones and her honey coloured skin shine up like mi coffee table, make mi heart swell with pride.

Mi house was in a very quiet area, and from de time mi did hear sey de street call Proverbs, mi did purchase de house. It had three bedrooms. Mi did have de front one, which could hold all mi things dem; a very large wardrobe which go from one corner to de next, a big big bed mi could bounce around in and still have room! Mi dressing table stretch from under one window to de next, yes it was a big room. Celeste bedroom was next door. Her room was half de size of mi own. She had a small wardrobe and single bed and one little chest of drawers she use as dressing table. De next room could just about hold mi. By de time mi stretch out mi hand so, and turn, de room full up. Now Celeste use dat room to do her exercise, it was just enough fi lift up her leg and spin round!

'Celeste, mi wish mi have more money so dat mi could build up extension on de back of de house, so yu could have a big big room fi sleep in and a next one fi dance in.'

Celeste would come and hug mi up, she was a good gal! 'Auntie, it's okay. My room is fine, it's big enough for me. Anyway, one day I'll be making enough money so that we can live in a bigger house with lots and lots of room,' she would say, kissing mi on mi head top.

'Oh, chile, where yu getting all dat kinda money from ee?' mi just laugh.

'Well, when I become a famous dancer, I'll be able to make lots of money.'

Mi smile. 'But tell mi, Celeste, yu not going fi dance all yur life, so yu have to start make some soon.' Mi just a jest, but Celeste turn serious pon mi.

'Auntie, I intend to dance for the rest of my life, and that's how I'll make my living and furthermore, nothing or no one will stop me and if they try, I'll kill them.' She get on de floor and do some exercise.

Yu know, life is funny. De way Celeste so thin it come in like she weak, dat's how people see her, but dat lickle girl have determination enough fi lift up de island of Jamaica outa de sea, with one hand. Hmm!

It was late spring, nearly summer, all de flowers dem a bloom, de grass look green and early morning de bird dem a sing out dem heart, right outside mi bedroom window, so mi get up early. When mi think back to dis particular time mi have fi blame miself somehow. Mi know dat sound hard, but mi did encourage Celeste. Yu see, mi love picknee. Mi never did get round fi have any miself, due to de fact of one wutless man mi did have fi run from, and so from dat mi did not want no more man! So, as mi was saying, whenever mi see picknee mi feel funny inside, no matter if mi out a street, or in de shops. So one morning when mi get up early and watch de television, mi see Lady Di have one lickle picknee bwoy, mi feel sad.

'Oh, look at de lickle picknee bwoy Lady Di have, look how she look at him,' mi sigh.

Celeste finish her exercise and a eat her bran (de bran taste awful it come in like punishment to eat it). 'Auntie, be patient, I'll have so many children one day you'll probably get fed up babysitting.'

Mi smile. 'Oh, no, darlin, mi love picknee. Yu could all have ten or even twenty, bring dem all to yur Auntie Wilima.' Mi well serious.

Celeste would laugh. 'Auntie, ten or twenty – I'd have no energy left to dance!'

Now, dat Florica start come to de house often. Mi granny sey people dat come to yur house often, a look fi something. Mi granny right. Florica come fi take Celeste out disco and party, but from de way she dress up fi kill, mi can see she a look man. But still, yu have fi understand dat mi mind was not so good at de time – it was full of picknee.

So Celeste start go out one time, two time, it come in regular dat she is out dancing every week. Mi never did mind, mi love fi see her dress up and enjoy herself.

Summer come. For a English summer it was very hot. All day long mi drinking ice water and just a take it easy. One Wednesday evening Celeste sey, 'Auntie sit down, I have something to tell you.' So mi sit down.

'Well, I've been meaning to tell you this for a while, but I wasn't sure myself, but, I think I am now. You see, I've met a young man...'

'Yes, yu have? Oh, mi so happy,' mi did ball out, mi so glad.

'Auntie wait, let me finish.' She was laughing. 'His name is Lowell, he's sooo handsome, he's a jeweller...'

'Him have money den...' Mi grin mi teeth.

'Auntie, don't be so materialistic, I'm not even sure, anyway, well, perhaps he might be...'

Mi start squealing. All mi could think bout was – picknee.

'All right, Auntie, seeing how you're not going to let me finish, I've invited him here for dinner on Friday.'

'Yes, tell him fi come.' Mi start fi plan out one big dinner fi cook him.

All Thursday mi looking in shop window at perambulator.

Mi start fi cook early Friday morning. Mi remember what mi granny say: 'Wilima, de sure way fi secure yur husband, is put plenty pepper in de meat, and plenty sugar pon de sweet.' Mi cut up some extra pepper in de meat pot, and shake in some black pepper seed on de fish – mi was making Solomon Gundy. Mi make one everlastingly big carrot cake, and pour some sweet, sweet syrup pon de top. Hmm, hmm.

Well by de time mi spin round and finish cook and dress up, Lowell come. At first mi wasn't too too sure whether dis bwoy was de right one fi mi niece. Him hair shave clean off with one thin line down de side fi him head. Him did have on one leather suit, de trousers so tight mi was surprise when mi hear him voice so low. Him did have one thick gold chain round him neck, it come in like toilet chain, and one big big gold ring on him finger, how him lift up him hand mi don't know.

But him did smell sweet, and when him shake mi hand, mi find him own more soft dan mine own! But she seem so happy, and de way him did eat like hog, mi was frightened dat de fish bone was going fi cut him palate. Mi never see him take out any bone out fi him mout, so mi suppose him did swallow dem. Him was a strong bwoy, because mi put so much pepper in de food, mi could just about eat it, in between two glass of ice water. Him have two large piece of carrot cake and lots of de sweet syrup, and him never once belch!

It was a nice dinner and all him could sey was, 'Auntie Wilima, that was fantastic. I'm surprised you haven't got a hundred men banging on your door. You're brilliant!' Mi just smile. Mi could see him did have manners and would treat Celeste and dem picknee good.

De only problem dat did hang over de whole evening was dat Florica did come. From mi understanding of de situation, she invite herself. Mi couldn't sey a thing until after dey both gone – which again mi never did think sey it was good fi Lowell fi drop home Florica. Mi start wash de dishes and Celeste was drying dem.

'Celeste, who invite Florica?'

'Oh, she just came along, she didn't have anything planned for the night.'

'So hmm, so she have bwoyfriend?'

'No, not really. She used to like Lowell quite a lot, but he was only prepared just to be friends with her, and now he loves me, she said she's happy he didn't have a girl that she didn't know. She's a good friend, Auntie.'

'Hmm, so mi see.'

All through de summer Lowell was always at de house. Him would drive up in one big red car, Celeste sey it was a Mercedes – mi never know about car. Mi just know him did drop mi to church one day and de way him a drive mi knew sey mi would be seeing mi Saviour soon.

As fi de gal Florica, she come to de house every living day. Mi never know how de young lovin couple put up with her, dem never have lickle time to demself. It start make mi think, what does dis gal want? Yu know, mi is a person who no like mystery. Mi like plain fact. Even when mi go school, if teacher say one thing, mi have fi question why and where and what. Mi granny say, 'Wilima, don't trouble trouble, till trouble trouble yu.' But mi never could help it, mi have fi know. Sometimes de way mi see people carry on, mi could all write one book.

Autumn come. All de leaves dem drop off right outside mi doorstep. Every day mi a sweep – come in like mi is street sweeper! Now dat de birds dem don't sing outside mi window, mi never get up so early.

It was a Saturday morning when Celeste burst into mi bedroom and jump pon mi bed, nearly bust de springs. 'Auntie, auntie, look!' She push some paper right under mi nose.

'How yu expect mi fi read dis, pass mi eyeglass!' But de way she a bounce and a carry on, mi could only read de top of de letter: 'Royal School of Ballet'.

'I've done it, I've done it, I'm in,' she bawl out loud.

'What yu sey?'

'Auntie, I've been accepted at the Royal School of Ballet, and I'm to start next autumn.'

'Yes, is so de letter sey. Oh mi dear, mi so happy fi yu.' Mi kiss and hug her.

By de time mi reach downstairs, Celeste is on de phone telling all de world she get in.

'Remember fi call yu mother, chile.'

She put her hand over de moutpiece. 'I've done it already,' she smile. Mi start fi fret bout how much de bill will be?

When Celeste come off de phone she was a lickle upset because something Florica sey to her. She did not want fi tell mi, but mi get it out of her. Imagine – Madam Florica tell Celeste sey she only get accept because dey want a 'token black'! Mi never know what she seying or meaning, mi just tell Celeste don't pay her no mind.

Anyhow dat evening Lowell come smelling sweet as usual. All him do is grin and sey, 'I'm right proud of you, babes. I knew you could do it!'

Him ask fi speak to mi. Yu know mi know what he was going to ask mi, mi could feel it in mi bones.

'Eh, Aunt Wilima, Celeste and I would like to get married.' Mi coulda cry.

'Oh yes!' Dat all mi could sey.

Yu know, it's not every man dese days dat want fi get married, and fi come and ask de family fi permission is such good manners, mi think to miself dat Celeste really marry a gentleman. But still yu know dis Florica business unsettle mi. She still a hang bout – so mi did encourage dem fi get married as soon as possible. Dem did – within a month. Mi sister never come to England – dey were having dem honeymoon in Jamaica. At de wedding it was mostly de young people dem and family. It was mi parson who marry dem.

Celeste look so beautiful and fresh, mi eye did run water, and de bridesmaids come in like angels. Lowell have on one suit dat did cost so much mi coulda build up mi extension, and Madam Florica have on one tight up dress mi start fi wonder how she manage fi breathe.

De reception was nice. Mi alone did all de cooking, and every last crumb did get eat off, none did leave. De sound system play some nice music; mi did get fed up with de reggae beat, but de young people dem like it. Lowell father was de Master of Ceremony, de man can chat! And every time him sey a few words him have fi drink a gallon of rum. By de time dem get to de final toast, de man could barely stand up. But all in all, everybody did enjoy demself.

Well de only sad thing at dat time was mi would now have fi live back by miself. Mi would really miss Celeste. She was moving into Lowell house in one posh district. De house was nice and big, it did have four good good size bedroom. It was only join up with one house next door, and it did have a verandah with big flowers pot on de ledge, running underneath de upstairs window.

When de young lovin couple was on honeymoon, mi was given de key fi check out de house all over, so dat if tief did come, mi would know what dem take – right. All over de house was one bouncy bouncy carpet, it come in like trampoline. In de front room was black leather furniture, mi woulda prefer a red flowers one instead, but de young people have different taste. De television was big like a cinema screen, mi enjoy watching mi favourite daytime programme.

Upstairs was beautiful, all de bedroom except fi one was de same size as mi own! In de young lovin couple bedroom was one everlastingly big kingsize bed! Dat was all. It did have one white silk bedspread. De bed was firm, just right fi mi back.

De bathroom make mi sigh. It was pink and white and yu have fi step up to de bath and den down into de bath tub. All de taps and things in gold. Mi dear, dem coulda invite Prince Charles and Lady Di fi de weekend and feel no shame.

Time wait fi no man. Before mi know it de young

lovin couple back! And winter nearly end. Celeste was teaching dancing and arrowbactics or something. She was getting herself ready fi go a ballet school. Mi did still wish fi picknee.

Mi love fi visit Celeste, her cooking not too bad, Lowell eat off everything anyway. But yu know, when mi did look at mi niece at dat time, her eye don't look so happy.

'Everything all right?'

'Yes, Auntie, no problems, everything's fine!' she sey.

Mi notice dat Florica would not come to de house when Lowell not dere. Mi never like mystery.

Lowell did purchase a new car. All him talk bout was dis car.

'Oh man, this car is wicked. It's like a plane on wheels.'

De car was de same red, it never look no different to mi.

Madam Florica could not stop talk bout it too: 'Oh Celeste, it's out of this world, you can't feel any bumps in the road, and as for speed, it's faster than electricity. It's wild!' She smile.

Celeste just smile back.

Mi was vex. Mi want fi know how Madam Florica know so much bout de car fi tell Celeste all bout it – when Lowell was Celeste husband?

Anyhow, all good things come to an end, mi dear. One evening mi just a relax in front of de television when de telephone ring. Mi nearly jump outa mi skin. 'Who coulda call mi now, ee?' From de time de man on de telephone sey, 'Doctor Jenkins from sucha such hospital', mi know something bad happen. It was Celeste and her husband involve inna one accident.

When mi first see Celeste wrap up in de bed in one

metal contraption, with drip in her arm and plaster on her leg, and bandage tie up her head, mi heart just feel like it coulda leap out of mi body.

'Celeste, Celeste, can yu hear me?'

Nothing. She never even open her eye.

'Celeste, Celeste, poor baby.' Mi feel eye water run down mi face.

'Auntie.' Dat was all mi hear at first. 'Auntie, is it really you?'

'Yes, baby, hush now.' Mi so please she can talk.

'It's okay, Auntie, I'm just tired. Can I have a sip of water, please?' Mi hold up her head and give her de water.

'Thank you, Auntie. Where's Lowell?'

'Him okay, Celeste. Celeste, what did happen?' Mi did have to know.

'Well, Auntie, as it's summertime I thought a day in the country would be nice ... I wasn't sure where to go, so my friend Gemma has a friend, whose friend ... ' – she get breathless, but from all dis friend business, mi know sey dat it not good – '... told me about this place called Beachy Head. How beautiful it was, with lots of hills and valleys, how wild blackberries and all different kind of things grew there ... how it was a good place to go and relax.' She tired, but Celeste still struggle fi finish tell mi.

'I really wanted Lowell to go because he works so hard in the shop.' Mi give her some more water. 'So we set off in the car. I sat in the back seat because I wanted to sleep, so Florica sat in the front.'

'Whaat!' mi shout. Mi did forget where mi was. 'How come Florica with yu both?'

'Well, Auntie, Florica wasn't doing anything that day, so Lowell asked her to come along.'

Dis really upset mi now mi know Madam Florica was dere. 'Anyhow, carry on, baby,' mi say.

'Lowell and Florica were...laughing and playing games.'

'How can yu play game and drive car?' mi ask Celeste.

'Auntie, I don't really know, you see I had fallen asleep, and when I woke up that's what they were doing. And then...' she nearly cry and mi feel so sad.

'It all right, Celeste, yu just sleep now.'

'But, but, Auntie, it was so terrible, all I can remember is the car going so fast, and Lowell was shouting that he couldn't control the wheel, and then we came off the road...suddenly, we were heading for an enormous tree. I started screaming and, and...' She crying real hard now. Mi start bawling too.

'Never mind, baby, mi have fi thank de Lawd yu is alive.' Eye water blind mi.

Mi so happy when Celeste come home, but it hurt mi fi see her inna wheelchair and now she not able fi go a ballet school. She hardly talk, just sit and stare. De hospital doctor sey dat Celeste spine bruise up so bad dem not sure how she going fi come out, and she have parralisis in her leg dem.

'We are uncertain as to whether she will ever gain full control of the use of her legs,' sey de doctor.

'But tell me something, doctor, how can yu sey dat, yu never know. Celeste was a ballet dancer and she need her leg dem, ee?'

'Well I'm sorry, but I can't be more specific. In such cases the permanence of the damage can only be determined in the course of time.' So Celeste might never walk again.

But what nearly kill mi was all dat Lowell do was lick

him head, him did all right and Madam Florica bruck her fingernail – dat was it!

Mi dear, mi did feel so murderous.

Mi try fi get to Celeste house every day, especially when mi hear sey Madam Florica did move in fi nurse Celeste. What she know bout nurse? In de day time dey both working, mi sit with Celeste.

One time mi did go a bathroom and Madam Florica room door open. Mi nearly fall down in shock at all de things she have pack in her room. Now Celeste tell mi dat Florica earn only a lickle money a week time, so how she manage fi buy all dese things? She never have bwoyfriend, and her mother and father nar rich, so how? Hmm, hmm.

What a way she have so much shoes! De box dem did pile up in one corner! When mi open de wardrobe and see so much clothes, mi have fi hang on to de door, mi feel so weak. She have one long long fancy fur coat, mi could not believe it. She have so much perfume bottle on de dressing table it come in like Boots de chemist!

Bwoy! Mi could not think straight. As mi walk downstairs mi wonder fi know if Celeste see all dat Florica have in her room. What a outrageous situation!

Mi did spend one Saturday evening with de lovin young couple and Madam Florica. Mi was surprise fi see one everlastingly gi-normous diamond ring, big like a duck egg, dat not even Elizabeth Taylor could wear, pon de wutless gal finger! Dis situation is very grave.

Mi did have fi ask Celeste later – after mi calm down – bout Florica and her room.

'Celeste, as mi walk pass Florica room, mi couldn't help notice dat she have how much clothes and shoes in her room, where she get dem from, ee?'

'Well, she says that she saves all her money, and then goes out on shopping sprees.'

'Hmm. But dat fur coat alone must take her all year fi save up and buy!'

Now even mi start lose lickle weight through de fretting. All dis things come in like a real mystery, but mi remember mi granny and she sey, 'Wilima, all dat glitter is not gold.' Mi granny so wise.

Christmas come round again so quick. Celeste no better, she just sit quiet in de wheelchair. All mi find miself a do is shop, soak some fruit fi bake cake, and go see Celeste. Coming from market one day, mi did feel fi see Celeste. Mi did still have de key, so mi let miself through de door. Mi rest mi bag down (dem still heavy even though mi only shopping fi one!). Mi call out; mi coulda hear some boom booming noise, and palam-pam music a beat out.

Mi slowly open up de front room door, Celeste was sitting in de armchair breathing hard, de wheelchair was on de other side of de room by de music system. Sweat was running down her face, and her chest justa heave in and out like when used she to do exercise. Her eye dem shining bright. De music was so loud – mi turn it off and put mi bag just inside de room.

'Celeste, yu all right?'

She sound breathless. 'Yes, Auntie, the music soothes me.'

'But – but it so loud?'

She smoothe down her hair. 'Eh, it's better for me when it's loud.'

Mi sigh. 'All right, be careful yu don't burst out yur eardrum. Want some tea?'

'Oh, yes please, Auntie!' She smile.

As mi come back with de tea, mi see Celeste reading de newspaper mi did bring with mi. But wait a minute, de wheelchair too far fi Celeste fi use, so mi wonder how she manage fi get it? But den mi have to ask miself if it was dere mi did leave de newspaper? But no, mi sure mi did leave it pon top of de television, and wait, how she get de packet of mint mi leave dere too? Hmm.

'Auntie, you really shouldn't carry those heavy shopping bags. Look, next time you come to see me straight from the market, get a cab and I'll pay for it.'

Mi nearly choke on de tea. 'Ee ee, all right, dear.' Mi shock. 'Ee Celeste, how you know sey mi bag dem heavy?' mi ask.

She never even look up from de newspaper. 'Oh, Auntie, I can see from the way you were carrying them that they're heavy.' Den she smile at me. Mi just smile back.

Mi think now is de time fi ask Celeste if she woulda do a lickle part-time work fi occupy her day.

'Well not really, and it's not as though we need the money. Lowell is worth quite a bit, what with the house and the shop and its contents – must be worth about half a million, Auntie.'

Mi could not believe dat dis young man coulda value so much. 'But dat is so much money, yu sure him worth it?'

'Well, from what I've seen of his policies, yes, I'm sure of the amount, but is he worth it...' De telephone ring. It just come in mi mind what mi granny would sey, 'De fish slip through de net!'

It funny, yu know, mi granny woulda see all what from what was going on. 'Wilima, what go round must come round,' mi coulda hear her sey it even now.

It did take half de year fi build up extension at de back of mi house. Every day see mi sweeping and dusting, but mi do have fi sey, de workmen did a good job. It did cost so much money but Celeste insist sey she will pay for everything.

Even de attic make into a next room. Now we live in a four bedroom mansion – imagine mi lickle house come out so big! It make it seem like a palace! But den, with mi, Celeste, her second husband and family living here, we need all de room possible. She look so fit and well now it hard fi mi fi even imagine how thin and sick she did look in de wheelchair all dat time ago.

'Celeste, mi can't stop look at you and thank de Lawd dat yu is now safe and well. Even de doctors have fi sey dat it a miracle how yu overcome de parralasis so well.' Celeste just smile.

'Oh, but Auntie, I do have you to thank for being so patient with me.'

'Dat a nothing chile, fi mi would do it fi stranger, how much more mi do it fi mi kin!'

'Auntie, that's a beautiful shawl you're crocheting. I'm so grateful to you.' Celeste rub her belly with her two picknee in it. 'You've crocheted so many things for me, you can stop when you like.'

'No, mi darlin. I like fi do it, especially fi mi grand-picknee dem.' Well, dem would be as good as grand-picknee, and mi will have dem all to miself when she go back fi take her dance class dem! When mi look at de picture fi Celeste and Nathan on dem wedding day, mi hardly think bout Lowell and Florica.

Yes dem did certainly find what dem was looking for.

Mi remember de day Celeste did tell me bout de whole situation as clear as water. At first she never sey a word, but mi have fi keep pushing her, cos it was pon her mind. Mi know what mi granny would sey: 'Goat mout have fi open fi fill him belly.' 'Celeste,' I sey to her, 'come tell yur auntie now.'

According to her, on dat fateful day, Lowell did promise fi take her out fi a drive. But him car did have some problem, so him decide fi fix it. All morning him busy fixing de car outside de garage. Celeste was sitting in de wheelchair upstairs on de verandah above de garage. Bout lunchtime Florica came back from de shop inna taxi. Celeste hear Florica coo: 'Lowell, poor thing, having to work on your car! Listen, I'll give you a hand.'

Now mi want fi know, how dis girl know bout car, come like she know about everything!

And Celeste sey, dat from de time Florica start help Lowell, no work get done. Dem justa fool round and laugh and stupidness. Celeste sey she wheel forward, lean over de verandah and shout out, 'Lowell, are you nearly finished, remember our drive out.'

'Babes,' him sey, 'Somehow I don't think we'll be going today, I won't be able to have the car done in time. Maybe tomorrow.'

Madam Florica shout out, 'Why don't you water the flowers, Celeste, that'll give you something to do.' She grin.

So Celeste sey, 'That's a good idea, Florica.'

Celeste hear Florica tell Lowell how she is going fi make lunch. 'I won't be a minute, darling.'

But stop! How can she call Lowell 'darling'! Celeste mout dry up and she stop talk, but in de end mi squeeze it out of her.

Poor Celeste was trying fi look bout de flowers and up till now she can't work out how it happen, because de flowers pot so heavy, but it seem de next thing she know, de flowers pot pon de verandah ledge fall down right where Lowell was fixing de car, and him get lick on him head top! Him fall down and not get up. By de time ambulance come and dey get him to hospital him dead. And by de time de police and everybody come Celeste in shock, she can't talk. Florica a bawl and scream, it come in like she turn mad. Yu see, she start lie bout how she see Celeste standing up, and how she musta pick up de heavy flowers pot and fling down on Lowell! Well dat is impossible, because Celeste could not stand, much less pick up heavy flowers pot and walk! Anyhow, Florica could not stop making noise, but everybody know how much she like fi chat foolishness, so de doctor advise her fi go on a holiday fi rest. And yu know, she must have had one holiday in a far place, cos we nar see her to dis day, praise de Lawd!

And yu know, it truly amazing: after one lickle while Celeste did meet up with Nathan, such a nice man, and before mi could blink mi eye, dem married!

When mi think back to how mi granny have answer to every living thing, it come in like a Solomon wisdom she did have. Yu know de shock fi Lowell death make Celeste walk – yes, life is funny. It was truly a blessing in disguise! Hmm, hmm, and as mi granny would sey, 'Today fi mi, tomorrow fi yu', and yu know – she right.

The Fruit at the Bottom of the Bowl

Ray Bradbury

Ray Bradbury

The Fruit at the Bottom of the Bowl

William Acton rose to his feet. The clock on the mantel ticked midnight.

He looked at his fingers and he looked at the large room around him and he looked at the man lying on the floor. William Acton, whose fingers had stroked typewriter keys and made love and fried ham and eggs for early breakfasts, had now accomplished a murder with those same ten whorled fingers.

He had never thought of himself as a sculptor and yet, in this moment, looking down between his hands at the body upon the polished hardwood floor, he realised that by some sculptural clenching and remodelling and twisting of human clay he had taken hold of this man named Donald Huxley and changed his physiognomy, the very frame of his body.

With a twist of his fingers he had wiped away the exacting glitter of Huxley's grey eyes; replaced it with a blind dullness of eye cold in socket. The lips, always pink and sensuous, were gaped to show the equine teeth, the yellow incisors, the nicotined canines, the gold-inlaid molars. The nose, pink also, was now mottled, pale, discoloured, as were the ears. Huxley's hands, upon the floor, were open, pleading for the first time in their lives, instead of demanding.

Yes, it was an artistic conception. On the whole, the change had done Huxley a share of good. Death made him a handsomer man to deal with. You could talk to him now and he'd have to listen.

William Acton looked at his own fingers.

It was done. He could not change it back. Had anyone heard? He listened. Outside, the normal late sounds of street traffic continued. There was no banging of the house door, no shoulder wrecking the portal into kindling, no voices demanding entrance. The murder, the sculpturing of clay from warmth to coldness was done, and nobody knew.

Now what? The clock ticked midnight. His every impulse exploded him in a hysteria towards the door. Rush, get away, run, never come back, board a train, hail a taxi, get, go, run, walk, saunter, but get the blazes *out* of here!

His hands hovered before his eyes, floating, turning.

He twisted them in slow deliberation; they felt airy and feather-light. Why was he staring at them this way, he inquired of himself; was there something in them of immense interest that he should pause now, after a successful throttling, and examine them whorl by whorl?

They were ordinary hands. Not thick, not thin, not long, not short, not hairy, not naked, not manicured and yet not dirty, not soft and yet not calloused, not wrinkled and yet not smooth; not murdering hands at all – and yet not innocent. He seemed to find them miracles to look upon.

It was not the hands as hands he was interested in, nor the fingers as fingers. In the numb timelessness after an accomplished violence he found interest only in the *tips* of his fingers.

The clock ticked upon the mantel.

He knelt by Huxley's body, took a handkerchief from Huxley's pocket, and began methodically to swab

Huxley's throat with it. He brushed and massaged the throat and wiped the face and the back of the neck with a fierce energy. Then he stood up.

He looked at the throat. He looked at the polished floor. He bent slowly and gave the floor a few dabs with the handkerchief, then he scowled and swabbed the floor; first, near the head of the corpse; secondly, near the arms. Then he polished the floor all around the body. He polished the floor one yard from the body on all sides. Then he polished the floor two yards from the body on all sides. Then he polished the floor three yards from the body in all directions. Then he . . . .

He stopped.

There was a moment when he saw the entire house, the mirrored halls, the carved doors, the splendid furniture; and, as clearly as if it were being repeated word for word, he heard Huxley· talking and himself talking just the way they had talked only an hour ago.

Finger on Huxley's doorbell. Huxley's door opening.

'Oh!' Huxley shocked. 'It's *you*, Acton.'

'Where's my wife, Huxley?'

'Do you think I'd tell you, really? Don't stand out there, you idiot. If you want to talk business, come in. Through that door. There. Into the library.'

Acton had *touched* the library door.

'Drink?'

'I need one. I can't believe Lily is gone, that she –'

'There's a bottle of burgundy, Acton. Mind fetching it from that cabinet?'

Yes, fetch it. *Handle* it. *Touch* it. He did.

'Some interesting first editions there, Acton. Feel this binding. *Feel* it.'

'I didn't come to see books, I . . .'

He had *touched* the books and the library table and

touched the burgundy bottle and the glasses.

Now, squatting on the floor beside Huxley's cold body with the polishing handkerchief in his fingers, motionless, he stared at the house, the walls, the furniture about him, his eyes widening, his mouth dropping, stunned by what he realised and what he saw. He shut his eyes, dropped his head, crushed the handkerchief between his hands, wadding it, biting his lips with his teeth, pulling in on himself.

The finger-prints were everywhere, *everywhere*!

'Mind getting the burgundy, Acton, eh? The burgundy bottle, eh? With your fingers, eh? I'm terribly tired. You understand?'

A pair of gloves.

Before he did one more thing, before he polished another area, he must have a pair of gloves, or he might unintentionally, after cleaning a surface, redistribute his identity.

He put his hands in his pockets. He walked through the house to the hall umbrella-stand, the hat-rack. Huxley's overcoat. He pulled out the overcoat pockets.

No gloves.

His hands in his pockets again, he walked upstairs, moving with a controlled swiftness, allowing himself nothing frantic, nothing wild. He had made the initial error of not wearing gloves (but, after all, he hadn't *planned* a murder, and his subconscious, which may have known of the crime before its commitment, had not even hinted he might need gloves before the night was finished), so now he had to sweat for his sin of omission. Somewhere in the house there must be at least one pair of gloves.

He would have to hurry; there was every chance that someone might visit Huxley, even at this hour. Rich friends drinking themselves in and out of the door, laughing, shouting, coming and going without so much as hullo-good-bye. He would have until six in the morning, at the outside, when Huxley's friends were to pick Huxley up for the trip to the airport and Mexico City . . . .

Acton hurried about upstairs opening drawers, using the handkerchief as blotter. He untidied seventy or eighty drawers in six rooms, left them with their tongues, so to speak, hanging out, ran on to new ones. He felt naked, unable to do anything until he found gloves. He might scour the entire house with the handkerchief, buffing every possible surface where fingerprints might lie, then accidentally bump a wall here or there, thus sealing his own fate with one microscopic, whorling symbol!

It would be putting his stamp of approval on the murder, that's what it would be! Like those waxen seals in the old days when they rattled parchment, flourished ink, dusted with sand to dry the ink, and pressed their signet-rings in hot crimson tallow at the bottom. So it would be if he left one, mind you, *one* fingerprint upon the scene! His approval of the murder did not extend as far as affixing said seal.

More drawers! Be quiet, be curious, be careful, he told himself.

At the bottom of the eighty-fifth drawer he found gloves.

'Oh, my lord!' He slumped against the bureau, sighing. He tried the gloves on, held them up, proudly flexed them, buttoned them. They were soft, grey, thick, impregnable. He could do all sorts of tricks with hands now and leave no trace. He thumbed his nose in the bedroom mirror, sucking his teeth.

'*No!*' cried Huxley.

What a wicked plan it had been.

Huxley had fallen to the floor, *purposely*! Oh, what a wickedly clever man! Down onto the hardwood floor had dropped Huxley, with Acton after him. They had rolled and tussled and clawed at the floor, printing and printing it with their frantic fingertips. Huxley had slipped away a few feet, Acton crawling after to lay hands on his neck and squeeze until the life came out like paste from a tube!

Gloved, William Acton returned to the room and knelt down upon the floor and laboriously began the task of swabbing every wildly infested inch of it. Inch by inch, inch by inch, he polished and polished until he could almost see his intent, sweating face in it. Then he came to a table and polished the leg of it, on up its solid body and along the knobs and over the top. He came to a bowl of wax fruit, burnished the filigree silver, plucked out the wax fruit and wiped them clean, leaving the fruit at the bottom unpolished.

'I'm sure I didn't touch *them*,' he said.

After rubbing the table, he came to a picture-frame hung over it. 'I'm certain I didn't touch *that*,' he said.

He stood looking at it. He glanced at all the doors in the room. Which doors had he used tonight? He couldn't remember. Polish all of them, then. He started on the door-knobs, shone them all up, and then he curried the doors from head to foot, taking no chances. Then he went to all the furniture in the room and wiped the chair arms.

'That chair you're sitting in, Acton, is an old Louis XIV piece. *Feel* that material,' said Huxley.

'I didn't come to talk furniture, Huxley! I came about Lily.'

'Oh, come off it, you're not that serious about

her. She doesn't love you, you know. She's told me she'll go with me to Mexico City tomorrow.'

'You and your money and your damned furniture!'

'It's nice furniture, Acton; be a good guest and feel it.'

Finger-prints can be found on fabric.

'Huxley!' William Acton stared at the body. 'Did you guess I was going to kill you? Did your subconscious suspect, just as my subconscious suspected? And did your subconscious tell you to make me run about the house handling, touching, *fondling* books, dishes, doors, chairs? Were you *that* clever and *that* mean?'

He washed the chairs dryly with the clenched handkerchief. Then he remembered the body – he hadn't dry-washed *it*. He went to it and turned it now this way, now that, and burnished every surface of it. He even shined the shoes, charging nothing. While shining the shoes his face took on a little tremor of worry, and after a moment he got up and walked over to that table.

He took out and polished the wax fruit at the bottom of the bowl. 'Better,' he whispered, and went back to the body.

But as he crouched over the body his eyelids twitched and his jaw moved from side to side and he debated, then he got up and walked once more to the table.

He polished the picture-frame. While polishing the picture-frame he discovered . . . .

The wall.

'That,' he said, 'is *silly*.'

'Oh!' Huxley had cried, fending him off. He gave Acton a shove as they struggled. Acton fell, got up, *touching* the wall, and ran towards Huxley again. He strangled Huxley. Huxley died.

Acton turned steadfastly from the wall, with equilibrium and decision. The harsh words and the action faded in his mind; he hid them away. He glanced at the four walls.

'Ridiculous!' he said.

From the corners of his eyes he saw something on one wall. 'I refuse to pay attention,' he said to distract himself. 'The next room, now! I'll be methodical. Let's see – altogether we were in the hall, the library, *this* room, and the dining-room and the kitchen.'

There was a spot on the wall behind him.

Well, *wasn't* there?

He turned angrily. 'All right, all right, just to be *sure*,' and he went over and couldn't find any spot. Oh, a *little* one, yes – right *there*. He dabbed it. It wasn't a finger-print, anyhow. He finished with it, and his gloved hand leaned against the wall and he looked at the wall and the way it went over to his right and over to his left and how it went down to his feet and up over his head and he said softly, 'No'. He looked up and down and over and across and he said quietly, 'That would be too much.' How many square feet? 'I don't give a damn,' he said. But unknown to his eyes, his gloved fingers moved in a little rubbing rhythm on the wall.

He peered at his hand and the wallpaper. He looked over his shoulder at the other room. 'I must go in there and polish the essentials,' he told himself, but his hand remained, as if to hold the wall, or himself, up. His face hardened.

Without a word he began to scrub the wall, up and down, back and forth, up and down, as high as he could stretch and as low as he could bend.

'Ridiculous, oh lord, ridiculous!'

But you must be certain, his thought said to him.

'Yes, one *must* be certain,' he replied.

He got one wall finished, and then . . . .

He came to another wall.

'What time *is* it?' He looked at the clock. An hour gone. It was five past one.

The doorbell rang.

Acton froze, staring at the door, the clock, the door, the clock.

Someone rapped loudly.

A long moment passed. Acton did not breathe. Without new air in his body he began to fail, to sway; his head roared a silence of cold waves thundering onto heavy rocks.

'Hey, in there!' cried a drunken voice. 'I know you're in there, Huxley! Open up, dammit! This is Billy-boy, drunk as an owl, Huxley, old pal, drunker than *two* owls.'

'Go away,' whispered Acton soundlessly, crushed against the wall.

'Huxley, you're in there, I hear you *breathing*!' cried the drunken voice.

'Yes, I'm in here,' whispered Acton, feeling long and sprawled and clumsy on the floor, clumsy and cold and silent. 'Yes.'

'Hell!' said the voice, fading away into mist. The footsteps shuffled off.

Acton stood a long time feeling the red heart beat inside his shut eyes, within his head. When at last he opened his eyes he looked at the new fresh wall straight ahead of him and finally got courage to speak. 'Silly,' he said. 'This wall's flawless. I won't touch it. Got to hurry. Got to hurry. Time, time. Only a few hours before those damn-fool friends blunder in!' He turned away.

From the corners of his eyes he saw the little webs. When his back was turned the little spiders came out of the woodwork and delicately spun their fragile little half-invisible webs. Not upon the wall at his left, which was already washed fresh, but upon the three walls as yet untouched. Each time he stared directly at them the spiders dropped back into the woodwork, only to spindle out as he retreated. 'Those walls are all right,' he insisted in a half-shout. 'I won't touch them!'

He went to a writing-desk at which Huxley had been seated earlier. He opened a drawer and took out what he was looking for. A little magnifying glass Huxley sometimes used for reading. He took the magnifier and approached the wall uneasily.

Finger-prints.

'But those aren't *mine*!' He laughed unsteadily. 'I didn't put them there! I'm sure I didn't! A servant, a butler, or a maid perhaps!'

The wall was full of them.

'Look at this one here,' he said. 'Long and tapered, a woman's, I'd bet money on it.'

Would you?

'I would!'

Are you certain?

'Yes!'

Positive!

'Well – yes.'

Absolutely?

'Yes, damn it, yes!'

Wipe it out: anyway: why don't you?

'There!'

Out damned spot, eh, Acton?

'And this one, over here,' scoffed Acton. 'That's the print of a fat man.'

Are you sure?

'Don't start *that* again!' he snapped, and rubbed it

out. He pulled off a glove and held his hand up, trembling, in the glaring light. 'Look at it, you idiot! See how the whorls go? See?'

That proves nothing!

'Oh, all right!' Raging, he swept the wall, up and down back and forth, with gloved hands, sweating, grunting, swearing, bending, rising, and getting redder of face.

He took off his coat, put it on a chair. 'Two o'clock,' he said, finishing the wall, glaring at the clock.

He walked over to the bowl and took out the wax fruit and polished the ones at the bottom and put them back, and polished the picture-frame.

He gazed up at the chandelier. His fingers twitched at his sides.

His mouth slipped open and the tongue moved along his lips and he looked at the chandelier and looked away and looked back at the the chandelier and looked at Huxley's body and then at the crystal chandelier with its long pearls of rainbow glass.

He got a chair and brought it over under the chandelier and put one foot up on it and took it down and threw the chair, violently, laughing, into a corner. Then he ran out of the room, leaving one wall as yet unwashed.

In the dining-room he came to a table.

'I want to show you my Georgian silver, Acton,' Huxley had said. Oh, that casual, that *hypnotic* voice!

'I haven't time,' Acton said. 'I've got to see Lily –'

'Nonsense, look at this silver, this exquisite craftsmanship.'

Acton paused over the table where the boxes of silver were laid out, hearing once more Huxley's voice, remembering all the touchings and gesturings.

Now Acton wiped the forks and spoons and took

down all the plaques and special porcelain dishes from
the wall shelf....

'Here's a lovely piece of china, Acton. Look!'

'It *is* lovely.'

'Pick it up. Turn it over. See the fine thinness of the
bowl, hand-thrown on a turn-table, thin as eggshell,
incredible. And the amazing volcanic glaze? Handle it,
go ahead. *I* don't mind.'

Handle it. Go ahead. Pick it up!

Acton sobbed unevenly. He hurled the bowl against
the wall. It shattered and spread, flaking wildly, upon
the floor.

An instant later he was on his knees. Every piece,
every shard of it, must be found. Fool, fool, fool! he
cried to himself, shaking his head and shutting and
opening his eyes and bending under the table. Find
every piece, idiot, not one fragment of it must be left
behind. Fool, fool! He gathered them. Are they all here?
He looked at them on the table before him. He looked
under the table again and under the chairs and the
service bureau and found one more piece by matchlight
and started to polish each little fragment as if it were a
precious stone. He laid them all out neatly upon the
shining polished table.

'A lovely bit of china, Acton. Go ahead – *handle* it.'

He took out the linen and wiped it and wiped the
chairs and tables and knobs and window-panes and
ledges and curtains, and wiped the floor, and found the
kitchen, panting, breathing violently, and took off his
vest and adjusted his gloves and wiped the glittering
chromium....

'I want to show you my house, Acton,' Huxley had
said. 'Come along....'

And he wiped all the utensils and the silver taps and
the mixing-bowls, for now he had forgotten what he had

touched and what he had not. Huxley and he had lingered here, in the kitchen, Huxley prideful of its array, covering his nervousness at the presence of a potential killer, perhaps wanting to be near the knives if they were needed. They had idled, touched this, that, something else — there was no remembering what or how much or how many. And he finished the kitchen and came through the hall into the room where Huxley lay.

He cried out. He had forgotten to wash the fourth wall of the room! And while he was gone the little spiders had popped from the fourth unwashed wall and swarmed over the already clean walls, dirtying them again! On the ceilings, from the chandelier, in the corners, on the floor, a million little whorled webs hung billowing at his scream! Tiny, tiny little webs, no bigger than, ironically, your – finger!

As he watched, the webs were woven over the picture-frame, the fruit bowl, the body, the floor. Prints wielded the paper-knife, pulled out drawers, touched the table-top, touched, touched, touched everything, everywhere.

He polished the floor wildly, wildly. He rolled the body over and cried on it while he washed it, and got up and walked over and polished the fruit at the bottom of the bowl. Then he put a chair under the chandelier and got up and polished each little hanging fire of it, shaking it like a crystal tambourine until it tilted bell-wise in the air.

Then he leapt off the chair and gripped the door-knobs and got up on other chairs and swabbed the walls higher and higher and ran to the kitchen and got a broom and wiped the webs down from the ceiling and polished the bottom fruit of the bowl and washed the body and door-knobs and silverware and found the hall banister and followed it upstairs.

Three o'clock! Everywhere, with a fierce, mechanical intensity, clocks ticked! There were twelve rooms downstairs and eight above. He worked out the yards and yards of space and time needed. One hundred chairs, six sofas, twenty-seven tables, six radios. He yanked furniture away from walls and, sobbing, wiped them clean of years-old dust, and staggered and followed the banister up, up the stairs, handling, erasing, rubbing, polishing, because if he left one little print it would reproduce and make a million more – and the job would have to be done all over again and now it was four o'clock!

And his arms ached and his eyes were swollen and he moved sluggishly about, on strange legs, his head down, his arms moving, swabbing and rubbing, bedroom by bedroom, closet by closet . . . .

They found him at six-thirty that morning. In the attic.

The entire house was polished to a brilliance. Vases shone like glass stars. Chairs were burnished. Bronzes, brasses, and coppers were all aglint. Floors sparkled. Banisters gleamed.

Everything glittered and shone, everything was bright!

They found him in the attic, polishing the old trunks and the old frames and the old chairs and the old carriages and toys and music-boxes and vases and cutlery and rocking-horses and dusty Civil War coins. He was half through the attic when the police officer walked up behind him with a gun.

'Done!'

On the way out of the house Acton polished the front door-knob with his handkerchief and slammed it in triumph!

Dick Francis

Twenty-one Good Men and True

Arnold Roper whistled breathily while he boiled his kettle and spooned instant own-brand economy pack coffee into the old blue souvenir from Brixham. Unmelodic and without rhythm, the whistling was nonetheless an expression of content, both with things in general and the immediate prospect ahead. Arnold Roper, as usual, was going to the races: and as usual, if he had a bet, he would win. Neat, methodical, professional, he would operate his unbeatable system and grow richer, the one following the other as surely as chickens and eggs.

Arnold Roper at forty-five was one of nature's bachelors, a lean-bodied, handy man accustomed to looking after himself, a man who found the chatter of companionship a nuisance. Like a sailor, though he had never been to sea, he kept his surroundings polished and ship-shape, ordering his life in plastic dustbin-liners and reheated take-away food.

The one mild problem on Arnold Roper's horizon was his wealth. The getting of the money was his most intense enjoyment. The spending of it was something he postponed to a remote and dreamlike future, when he would exchange his sterile flat for a warm, unending idyll under tropical palms. It was the interim storage of the money which was currently causing him, if not positive worry, at least occasional frowns of doubt. He might, he thought, as he stirred dried milk grains into the brownish brew, have to find space for yet another wardrobe in his already crowded bedroom.

If anyone had told Arnold Roper he was a miser he would have denied it indignantly. True, he lived frugally, but by habit rather than obsession: and he never took out his wealth just to look at it, and count, and gloat. He would not have admitted as miserliness the warm feeling that stole over him every night as he lay down to sleep, smiling from the knowledge that all around him, filling two oak-veneered sale-bargain bedroom suites, was a ton or two of negotiable paper.

It was not that Arnold Roper distrusted banks. He knew, too, that money won by betting could not be lost by tax. He would not have kept his growing gains physically around him were it not that his unbeatable system was also a splendid fraud.

The best frauds are only ever discovered by accident, and Arnold could not envisage any such accident happening to *him*.

Jamie Finland woke to his customary darkness and thought three disconnected thoughts with the first second of consciousness. The sun is shining. It is Wednesday. They are racing today here at Ascot.

He stretched out a hand and put his fingers delicately down on the top of his bedside tape recorder. There was a cassette lying there. Jamie smiled, slid the cassette into the recorder, and switched on.

His mother's voice spoke to him. 'Jamie, don't forget the man is coming to mend the television at ten-thirty and please put the washing into the machine, there's a dear, as I am so pushed this morning, and would you mind having yesterday's soup again for lunch. I've left it in a saucepan ready. Don't lose all that ten quid this afternoon or I'll cut the plug off your stereo. Home soon after eight, love.'

Jamie Finland's thirty-eight-year-old mother supported them both on her earnings as an agency nurse, and she had made a fair job, her son considered, of bringing up a child who could not see. He rose gracefully from bed and put on his clothes: blue shirt, blue jeans. 'Blue is Jamie's favourite colour,' his mother would say, and her friends would say 'Oh yes?' politely and she could see them thinking 'How could he possibly know?' But Jamie could identify blue as surely as his mother's voice, and red, and yellow, and every colour in the spectrum, as long as it was daylight. 'I can't see in the dark,' he had said when he was six, and only his mother, from watching his sureness by day and his stumbling by night, had understood what he meant. Walking radar, she called him. Like many young blind people he could sense the wave-length of light, and distinguish the infinitesimal changes of frequency reflected from coloured things close to him. Strangers thought him uncanny. Jamie believed everyone could see that way if they wanted to, and could not himself clearly understand what they meant by sight.

He made and ate some toast and thankfully opened the door to the television fixer. 'In my room,' he said, leading the way. 'We've got sound but no picture.' The television fixer looked at the blind eyes and shrugged. If the boy wanted a picture he was entitled to it, same as everyone else who paid their rental. 'Have to take it back to the workshop,' he said, judicially pressing buttons.

'The races are on,' Jamie said. 'Can you fix it by then?'

'Races? Oh yeah. Well . . . Tell you what, I'll lend you another set. Got one in the van . . .' He staggered off with the invalid and returned with the replacement. 'Not short of radios, are you,' he said, looking around. 'What do you want six for?'

'I leave them tuned to different things,' Jamie said. 'That one,' he pointed accurately, 'listens to aircraft, that one to the police, those three are on ordinary radio stations, and this one . . . local broadcasts.'

'What you need is a transmitter. Put you in touch with all the world.'

'I'm working on it,' Jamie said. 'Starting today.'

He closed the door after the man and wondered whether betting on a certainty was in itself a crime.

Greg Simpson had no such qualms. He paid his way into the Ascot paddock, bought a racecard, and ambled off to add a beer and sandwich to a comfortable paunch. Two years now, he thought, munching, since he had first set foot on the Turf: two years since he had exchanged his principles for prosperity and been released from paralysing depression. They seemed a distant memory, now, those fifteen months in the wilderness; the awful humiliating collapse of his seemingly secure pensionable world. No comfort in knowing that mergers and cutbacks had thrown countless near-top managers like himself onto the redundancy heap. At fifty-two, with long success-strewn experience and genuine administrative skill, he had expected that he at least would find another suitable post easily; but door after closed door, and a regretful chorus of 'Sorry, Greg,' 'Sorry, old chap,' 'Sorry, Mr Simpson, we need someone younger,' had finally thrust him into agonised despair. And it was just when, in spite of all their anxious economies, his wife had had to deny their two children even the money to go swimming, that he had seen the curious advertisement.

Jobs offered to mature respectable persons who must have been unwillingly unemployed for at least twelve months.

Part of his mind told him he was being invited to commit a crime, but he had gone nonetheless to the subsequently arranged interview, in a London pub, and he had been relieved, after all, to meet the very ordinary man holding out salvation. A man like himself, middle-aged, middle-educated, wearing a suit and tie and indoor skin.

'Do you go to the races?' Arnold Roper asked. 'Do you gamble? Do you follow the horses?'

'No,' Greg Simpson said prudishly, seeing the job prospect disappear but feeling all the same superior. 'I'm afraid not.'

'Do you bet on dogs? Go to Bingo? Do the Pools? Play bridge? Feel attracted by roulette?'

Greg Simpson silently shook his head and prepared to leave.

'Good,' said Arnold Roper cheerfully. 'Gamblers are no good to me. Not for this job.'

Greg Simpson relaxed into a glow of self-congratulation on his own virtue. 'What job?' he said.

Arnold Roper wiped out the Simpson smirk. 'Going to the races,' he said bluntly. 'Betting when I say bet, and never at any other time. You would have to go to race meetings most days, like any other job. You would be betting on certainties, and after every win I would expect you to send me twenty-five pounds. Anything you made above that would be yours. It is foolproof, and safe. If you go about it in a businesslike way, and don't get tempted into the mug's game of backing your own fancy, you'll do very well. Think it over. If you're interested, meet me here again tomorrow.'

Betting on certainties ... every one a winner. Arnold Roper had been as good as his word, and Greg Simpson's lifestyle had returned to normal. His qualms had evaporated once he learned that even if the fraud were discovered, he himself would not be involved. He did not know how his employer acquired his infallible information, and, if he speculated, he didn't ask. He knew him only as John Smith, and had never met him since those first two days, but he heeded his warning that if he failed to attend the specified race meetings or failed to send his twenty-five payment, the bounty would stop dead.

He finished his sandwich and went down to mingle with the bookmakers as the horses cantered down to the post for the start of the first race.

From high on the stands Arnold Roper looked down through powerful binoculars, spotting his men one by one. The perfect workforce, he thought, smiling to himself; no absenteeism, no union troubles, no complaints. There were twenty-one of them at present on his register, all contentedly receiving his information, all dutifully returning their moderate levies, and none of them knowing of the existence of the others. In an average week they would all bet for him twice; in an average week, after expenses, he added a thousand in readies to his bedroom.

In the five years since he had begun in a small way to put his scheme into operation, he had never picked a defaulter. The thinking-it-over time gave the timid and the honest an easy way out; and if Arnold himself had doubts, he simply failed to return on day two. The rest, added one by one to the fold, lived comfortably with quiet minds and prayed that their benefactor would never be rumbled.

Arnold himself couldn't see why he ever should be. He put down the binoculars and began in his methodical fashion to get on with his day's work. There was always a good deal to see to in the way of filling in forms, testing equipment, and checking that the nearby telephone was working. Arnold never left anything to chance.

Down at the starting gate sixteen two-year-olds bucked and skittered as they were fed by the handlers into the stalls. Two-year-old colts, thought the starter resignedly, looking at his watch, could behave like a pack of prima donnas in a heatwave in Milan. If they didn't hurry with that chestnut at present squealing and backing away determinedly, he would let the other runners off without him. He was all too aware of the television cameras pointing his way, mercilessly awaiting his smallest error. Starters who got the races off minutes late were unpopular. Starters who got the races off early were asking for official reprimands and universal curses, because of the fiddles that had been worked in the past on premature departures.

The starter ruled the chestnut out of the race and pulled his lever at time plus three minutes twenty seconds, entering the figures meticulously in his records. The gates crashed open, the fifteen remaining colts roared out of the stalls, and along on the stands the serried ranks of race-glasses followed their progress over the five-furlong sprint.

Alone in his special box, the judge watched intently. A big pack of two-year-olds over five furlongs were often a problem, presenting occasionally even to his practised eyes a multiple dead heat. He had learned all the horses by name and all the colours by heart, a chore he shared every day with the race-reading commentators, and from long acquaintance he could recognise most of the jockeys by their riding style alone, but still the ignominy of making a mistake flitted uneasily through his dreams. He squeezed his eyeballs, and concentrated.

Up in his eyrie the television commentator looked through his high-magnification binoculars, which were mounted rocksteady like a telescope, and spoke unhurriedly into his microphone: 'Among the early leaders are Breakaway and Middle Park, followed closely by Pickup, Jetset, Darling Boy and Gumshoe . . . Coming to the furlong marker the leaders are bunched, with Jetset, Darling Boy, Breakaway all showing . . . One furlong out, there is nothing to choose between Darling Boy, Jetset, Gumshoe, Pickup . . . In the last hundred yards . . . Jetset, Darling Boy . . .'

The colts stretched their necks, the jockeys swung their whips, the crowd rose on tiptoes and yelled in a roar which drowned the commentary, and in his box the judge's eyes ached with effort. Darling Boy, Jetset, Gumshoe and Pickup swept past the winning post in line abreast, and an impersonal voice over the widespread loudspeakers announced calmly, 'Photograph. Photograph.'

Half a mile away in his own room Jamie Finland listened to the race on television and tried to imagine the pictures on the screen. Racing was misty to him. He knew the shape of the horses from handling toys and riding a rocker, but their size and speed were mysterious; he had no conception at all of a broad sweep of railed racecourse, or of the size or appearance of trees.

As he grew older, Jamie was increasingly aware that he had drawn lucky in the maternal stakes, and he had become in his teens protective rather than rebellious, which touched his hard-pressed mother sometimes to tears. It was for her sake that he had welcomed the television fixer, knowing that, for her, sound without pictures was almost as bad as pictures without sound for himself. Despite a lot of trying he could pick up little from the screen through his ultra-sensitive fingertips. Electronically produced colours gave him none of the vibrations of natural light.

He sat hunched with tension at his table, the telephone beside his right hand and one of his radios at his left. There was no telling, he thought, whether the bizarre thing would happen again, but if it did, he would be ready.

'One furlong out, nothing to choose...' said the television commentator, his voice rising to excitement-inducing crescendo. 'In the last hundred yards, Jetset, Darling Boy, Pickup and Gumshoe... At the post, all in line... perhaps Pickup got there in the last stride but we'll have to wait for the photograph. Meanwhile, let's see the closing stages of the race again...'

The television went back on its track, and Jamie waited intently with his fingers over the quick easy numbers of the push-button telephone.

Along on the racecourse the crowds buzzed like agitated bees round the bookmakers who were transacting deals as fast as they could. Photo-finishes were always popular with serious gamblers, who bet with fervour on the outcome. Some punters really believed in the evidence of their own quick eyes: others found it a chance to hedge their main bet or even recoup a positive loss. A photo was the second chance, the lifebelt to the drowning, the temporary reprieve from torn-up tickets and anti-climax.

'Six-to-four on Pickup,' shouted young Billy Hitchins hoarsely, from his prime bookmaking pitch in the front row facing the stands, 'Six-to-four on, Pickup.' A rush of customers descending from the crowded steps enveloped him. 'A tenner, Pickup, right sir. Five on Gumshoe, right sir. Twenty Pickup, you're on sir, Fifty? Yeah, if you like. Fifty at evens, Jetset, why not...' Billy Hitchins, in whose opinion Darling Boy had taken the race by a nostril, was happy to rake in the money.

Greg·Simpson accepted Billy Hitchins' ticket for an even fifty on Jetset and hurried to repeat his bet with as many bookmakers as he could reach. There was never much time between the arrival of the knowledge and the announcement of the winner. Never much, but always enough. Two minutes at least. Sometimes as much as five. A determined punter could strike five or six bets in that time, given a thick skin and a ruthless use of elbows. Greg reckoned he could burrow to the front of the closest of throngs after all those years of rush-hour commuting on the Underground, and he managed, that day at Ascot, to lay out all the cash he had brought with him; all four hundred pounds of it, all at evens, all on Jetset.

Neither Billy Hitchins, nor any of his colleagues, felt the slightest twinge of suspicion. Sure, there was a lot of support for Jetset, but so there was for the three other horses, and in a multiple finish like this one a good deal of money always changed hands. Billy Hitchins welcomed it, because it gave him, too, a chance of making a second profit on the race.

Greg noticed one or two others scurrying with wads to Jetset, and wondered, not for the first time, if they too were working for Mr Smith. He was sure he'd seen them often at other meetings, but he felt no inclination at all to accost one of them, and ask. Safety lay in anonymity; for him, for them, and for John Smith.

In his box the judge pored earnestly over the black-and-white print, sorting out which nose belonged to Darling Boy, and which to Pickup. He could discern the winner easily enough, and had murmured its number aloud as he wrote it on the pad beside him. The microphone linked to the public announcement system waited mutely at his elbow for him to make his decision on second and third places, a task seeming increasingly difficult. Number two, or number eight. But which was which?

It was quiet in his box, the scurrying and shouting among the bookmakers' stands below hardly reached him through the window glass.

At his shoulder a racecourse official waited patiently, his job only to make the actual announcement, once the decision was made. With a bright light and a magnifying glass the judge studied the noses. If he got them wrong, a thousand knowledgeable photo-readers would let him know it. He wondered if he should see about a new prescription for his glasses. Photographs never seemed so sharp in outline these days.

Greg Simpson thought regretfully that the judge was overdoing the delay. If he had known he would have had so much time, he would have brought with him more than four hundred. Still, four hundred clear profit (less betting tax) was a fine afternoon's work; and he would send Mr Smith his meagre twenty-five with a grateful heart. Greg Simpson smiled contentedly, and briefly, as if touching a lucky talisman, he fingered the tiny transistorised hearing aid he wore unobtrusively under hair and trilby behind his left ear.

Jamie Finland listened intently, head bent, his curling dark hair falling on to the radio with which he eavesdropped on aircraft. The faint hiss of the carrier wave reached him unchanged, but he waited with quickening pulse and a fluttering feeling of excitement. If it didn't happen, he thought briefly, it would be very boring indeed.

Although he was nerve-strainingly prepared, he almost missed it. The radio spoke one single word, distantly, faintly, without emphasis, 'Eleven'. The carrier wave hissed on, as if never disturbed, and it took Jamie's brain two whole seconds to light up with a laugh of joy.

He pressed the buttons and connected himself to the local book-making firm.

'Hullo? This is Jamie Finland. I have a ten pound credit arranged with you for this afternoon. Well... please will you put it all on the result of the photo-finish of this race they've just run at Ascot? On number eleven, please.'

'Eleven?' echoed a matter-of-fact voice at the other end. 'Jetset?'

'That's right,' Jamie said. 'Eleven. Jetset.'

'Right. Jamie Finland, even tenner on Jetset. Right?'

'Right,' Jamie said. 'I was watching it on the box.'

'Don't we all, chum,' said the voice in farewell, clicking off.

Jamie sat back in his chair with a tingling feeling of mischief. If eleven really had won, he was surely plain robbing the bookie. But who would know? How could anyone ever know? He wouldn't even tell his mother, because she would disapprove and might make him give the winnings back. He imagined her voice if she came home and found he had turned her ten pounds into twenty. He also imagined it if she found he had lost it all on the first race betting on the result of a photo-finish that he couldn't even see.

He hadn't told her that it was because of the numbers on the radio he had wanted to bet at all. He'd said that he knew people often bet from home while they were watching racing on television. He'd said it would give him a marvellous new interest, if he could do that while she was out at work. He had persuaded her without much trouble to lend him a stake and arrange things with the bookmakers, and he wouldn't have done it at all if the certainty factor had been missing.

When he'd first been given the radio which received aircraft frequencies he had spent hours and days listening to the calls of the jetliners thundering overhead on their way in and out of Heathrow; but the fascination had worn off, and gradually he tuned in less and less. By accident one day, having twiddled the tuning knob aimlessly without finding an interesting channel, he forgot to switch the set off. In the afternoon, while he was listening to the Ascot televised races, the radio suddenly emitted one word. 'Twenty-three.'

Jamie switched the set off but took little real notice until the television commentator, announcing the result of the photo-finish, spoke almost as if in echo. 'Twenty-three . . . Swanlake, number twenty-three, is the winner.'

How *odd* Jamie thought. He left the tuning knob undisturbed, and switched the aircraft radio on again the following Saturday, along with Kempton Park races on television. There were two photo-finishes, but no voice-of-God on the ether. Ditto nil results from Doncaster, Chepstow and Epsom persuaded him, shrugging, to put it down to coincidence, but with the re-arrival of a meeting at Ascot he decided to give it one more try.

'Five,' said the radio quietly; and later 'ten'. And, duly, numbers five and ten were given the verdict by the judge.

The judge, deciding he could put off the moment no longer, handed his written down result to the waiting official, who leaned forward and drew the microphone to his mouth.

'First, number eleven,' he said. 'A dead heat for second place between number two and number eight. First Jetset. Dead heat for second, Darling Boy and Pickup. The distance between first and second a short head. The fourth horse was number twelve.'

The judge leaned back in his chair and wiped the sweat from his forehead. Another photo-finish safely past ... but there was no doubt they were testing to his nerves.

Arnold Roper picked up his binoculars the better to see the winning punters collect from the bookmakers. His twenty-one trusty men had certainly had time today for a thorough killing. Greg Simpson, in particular, was sucking honey all along the line; but then Greg Simpson, with his outstanding managerial skills, was always, in Arnold's view, the one most likely to do best. Greg's success was as pleasing to Arnold as his own.

Billy Hitchins handed Greg his winnings without a second glance, and paid out, too, to five others whose transistor hearing aids were safely hidden by hair. He reckoned he had lost, altogether, on the photo betting, but his book for the race itself had been robustly healthy. Billy Hitchins, not displeased, switched his mind attentively to the next event.

Jamie Finland laughed aloud and banged his table with an ecstatic fist. Someone, somewhere, was talking through an open microphone, and if Jamie had had the luck to pick up the transmission, why shouldn't he? Why shouldn't he? He thought of the information as an accident, not a fraud, and he waited with uncomplicated pleasure for another bunch of horses to finish nose to nose. Betting on certainties, he decided, quietening his conscience, was not a crime if you come by the information innocently.

After the fourth race he telephoned to bet on number fifteen, increasing his winnings to thirty-five pounds.

Greg Simpson went home at the end of the afternoon with a personal storage problem almost as pressing as Arnold's. There was a limit, he discovered, to the amount of ready cash one could stow away in an ordinary suit, and he finally had to wrap the stuff in the *Sporting Life* and carry it home under his arm, like fish and chips. Two in one day, he thought warmly. A real clean-up. A day to remember. And there was always tomorrow, back here at Ascot, and Saturday at Sandown, and next week, according to the list which had arrived anonymously on the usual postcard, Newbury and Windsor. With a bit of luck he could soon afford a new car, and Joan could book up for the skiing holiday with the children.

Billy Hitchins packed away his stand and equipment, and with the help of his clerk carried them the half mile along the road to his betting shop in Ascot High Street. Billy at eighteen had horrified his teachers by ducking university and apprenticing his bright mathematical brain to his local bookie. Billy at twenty-four had taken over the business, and now, three years later, was poised for expansion. He had had a good day on the whole, and after totting up the total, and locking the safe, he took his betting-shop manager along to the pub.

'Funny thing,' said the manager over the second beer. 'That new account, the one you fixed up yesterday, with that nurse.'

'Oh yes... the nurse. Gave me ten quid in advance. They don't often do that.' He drank his scotch and water.

'Yeah... Well, this Finland, while he was watching the telly, he phoned in two bets, both on the results of the photos, and he got it right both times.'

'Can't have that,' said Billy, with mock severity.

'He didn't place other bets, see? Unusual, that.'

'What did you say his name was?'

'Jamie Finland.'

The barmaid leaned towards them over the bar, her friendly face smiling and the pink sweater leaving little to the imagination. 'Jamie Finland?' she said. 'Ever such a nice boy, isn't he? Shame about him being blind.'

'What?' said Billy.

The barmaid nodded. 'Him and his mother, they live just down the road in those new flats, next door to my sister. He stays home most of the time, studying and listening to his radios. And you'd never believe it, but he can tell colours, he can really. My sister says it's really weird, but he told her she was wearing a green coat, and she was.'

'I don't believe it,' Billy said.

'It's true as God's my judge,' said the barmaid, offended.

'No...' Billy said. 'I don't believe that even if he can tell a green coat from a red he could distinguish colours on a television screen with three or four horses crossing the line abreast. You can't do it often even if you can see.' He sat and thought. 'It could be a coincidence,' he said. 'On the other hand, I lost a lot today on those photos.' He thought longer. 'We all took a caning over those photos.' I heard several of the other bookies complaining about the run on Jetset...' He frowned. 'I don't see how it could be rigged...'

Billy put his glass down with a crash which startled the whole bar.

'Did you say Jamie Finland listens to radios? What radios?'

'How should I know?' said the barmaid, bridling.

'He lives near the course,' Billy said, thinking feverishly. 'So just suppose he somehow overheard the photo result before it was given on the loudspeakers. But that doesn't explain the delay...how there was time for him...and probably quite a lot of others who heard the same thing...to get their money on.'

'I don't know what you're on about,' said the barmaid.

'I think I'll pop along and see Jamie Finland,' said Billy Hitchins. 'And ask who or what he heard...if he heard anything at all...'

'Bit far-fetched,' said the manager judiciously, 'The only person who could delay things long enough would be the judge.'

'Oh my God,' said Billy, awestruck. 'What about that? What about the judge?'

Arnold Roper did not know about the long fuse being lit in the pub. To Arnold, Billy Hitchins was a name on a bookmaker's stand. He could not suppose that brainy Billy Hitchins would drink in a pub where the barmaid had a sister who lived next door to a blind boy who had picked up his discreet transmissions on a carelessly left-on radio which, unlike most, was capable of receiving one-ten to one-forty megahertz on V.H.F.

Arnold Roper travelled serenely homewards with his walkie-talkie type transmitter hidden as usual inside his inner jacket pocket, its short aerial retracted now safely out of sight. The line-of-sight low-powered frequency he used was in his opinion completely safe, as only a passing aircraft was likely to receive it, and no pilot on earth would connect a simple number spoken on the air with the winner of the photo-finish down at Ascot, or Epsom, or Newmarket, or York.

Back on the racecourse Arnold had carefully packed away and securely locked up the extremely delicate and expensive apparatus which belonged to the firm which employed him. Arnold Roper was not the judge. Arnold Roper's job lay in operating the photo-finish camera. It was he who watched the print develop; he who could take his time delivering it to the judge; he who always knew the winner first.

Butchers

Peter Lovesey

Peter Lovesey

Butchers

He had passed the weekend in the cold store of Pugh the butcher's. It was now Monday morning. The door was still shut. He was unconcerned. Quite early on Saturday evening he had given up beating his fists on the door and screaming for help. He had soon tired of jumping and arm-swinging to keep his circulation going. He had become increasingly drowsy as his brain had succumbed to the deprivation of óxygen. He had lain on the tiled floor below the glistening carcases and by Sunday morning he had frozen to death.

On the other side of the door Joe Wilkins filled two mugs with instant coffee. It was still only 8 a.m. and the shop didn't open until 8.30. He was Mr Pugh's shop manager, forty-four, a master butcher, dark, good-looking with an old-fashioned Clark Gable moustache and quick, laughing eyes that had a way of involving everyone in the shop each time he passed a joke with a customer.

The second mug was for Frank, the apprentice butcher. Frank was eighteen and useful for heavy work. He earned extra money on Saturday nights as a bouncer in Stacey's, the disco across the street. When the deliveries came from the slaughterer's, Frank would take sides of beef on his back as if they were pieces of polystyrene. The girls from Woolworth's next door often came into the shop in their lunch-hour and asked Frank for rides on his motorbike. Frank got embarrassed when Joe Wilkins teased him about it.

Frank hung up his leather jacket and put on a clean apron. Joe was already wearing his straw boater. He watched the young man struggle awkwardly with the apron strings, tying a bow so loose that it was sure to fall apart as soon as he stretched up to lift a carcase off its hook.

'Another heavy weekend, lad?'

'Not really,' answered Frank, taking his coffee and slopping some on the chopping block. 'Same as usual.'

'That's good to hear. Looks as if we've got a busy morning ahead of us.'

Frank gave a frown.

Joe snapped his fingers. 'Come on, lad, what's different this morning, or haven't you noticed yet?'

Frank looked around the shop. 'Meat's not out yet.'

'Right! And why not?'

'Percy isn't in.'

'Right again. By Jove, I was wrong about you. You ought to be on the telly with a mind as sharp as that. Why spend the rest of your life hacking at pieces of meat when you could earn millions sitting in an armchair answering questions? And now for five hundred and a holiday for two in the Bahamas, Mr Dobson, what do you think has happened to Percy?'

'Dunno,' answered Frank.

'You don't know? Come on, lad. You're not trying.'

'He could have fallen off his bike again.'

'That's more like it,' said Joe as he took his knives and cleavers from the drawer behind the counter and started sharpening them. 'Get the window ready, will you?'

Frank put down his coffee and looked for the enamel trays that usually stood in the shop window.

Joe said, 'You're probably right about Percy. He's too old to be in charge of a bike. Seven miles is a long way on a morning like this, with ice all the way up Bread and Cheese Hill and the motorists driving like lunatics. He was knocked in the ditch last week, poor old devil.'

'Where does he put the trays?' asked Frank.

'Trays?'

'For the meat – in the window.'

'Aren't they there, then?' Joe put down his knife and went to look. 'Well, I never noticed that before. I suppose he puts them away somewhere. By the time I arrive, they're always here. Have a look behind the deep-freeze cabinet. Got 'em? Good. Blowed if I understand why he bothers to do that.'

'Dust, I expect,' said Frank.

'Quite right. Wipe them over with a cloth, lad. I used to wonder what he did with himself before we arrived in the morning. He's in by six, you know, regular. How about that? He must be up at five. Could you do that six mornings a week? And it gets no easier as you get older. Percy must be pushing seventy by now.'

'What *does* he do before we get in?' asked Frank.

'Well, it's always spotless, isn't it?'

'I thought that was because he stays on of a night to clean up after we close.'

'So he does – but there's always more dust by the morning. Percy wipes all the surfaces clean. He puts out the trays, and the cuts from the cold store, and hangs up the poultry, and opens a tin of liver and checks everything against the price list and puts out the tags and the plastic parsley, and the new-laid eggs and the packets of stuffing and bread sauce. I hope you're listening, lad, because I want all those jobs done before we open.'

146

Frank gave another frown. 'You want me to do all that?'

'Who else, lad?' said Joe in a reasonable voice. 'It's obvious that Percy isn't going to make it this morning, and I've got the orders to get out.'

'He hasn't had a day off since I started last year,' said Frank, still unable to believe his bad luck.

'He hasn't had a day off in the twenty years I've been working here. Six in the morning till seven at night, six days a week. And what for? Boy's work. He does the work you ought to be doing, lad. No one else but Percy would stand for it. Fetching and carrying and sweeping up. Do you know, he's never once complained to me or Mr Pugh or anyone else. You've seen him bent nearly double carrying in the carcases. A man of his age shouldn't be doing work like that. It's exploitation, that's what it is.'

'Why does he do it, then? He's old enough to draw his pension.'

Joe shook his head. 'He wouldn't be happy with his feet up. He's spent the best years of his life working in this shop. He was here before Mr Pugh took it over. It was Slater's in those days. Yes, Percy can tell you some tales about the old days. It means a lot to him, working in this shop.'

Frank gave a shrug and went to the cold store to get out the small joints left over from Saturday. The cold store consisted of two chambers, one for the chilled meat, the other for the frozen. He opened the door of the chiller and started taking out legs of lamb. He needed to hurry to fill the trays in the window by opening time.

Joe was still sharpening knives. He continued telling Frank about the injustices heaped on Percy. 'He gets no recognition for all the work he puts in. Blind loyalty, I call it, but there are some that would call it plain stupidity. Do you think Mr Pugh appreciates what Percy does? Of course he doesn't.'

'He's never here, is he?' contributed Frank, who was becoming quite skilful at fuelling Joe's maledictions against their employer.

'That's a fact. To be fair to Mr Pugh, he has to look in at the market and collect the meat from the slaughter-house, but that shouldn't take all day. It wouldn't hurt him to show his face here more often.'

Frank gave a sly grin. 'It might hurt someone else.'

'What do you mean by that?' asked Joe, taking offence.

'Well, you and me. We don't want the boss breathing down our necks, do we?'

Joe said in a curt tone, 'Speak for yourself, boy. I'm not ashamed of my work.' He put down the knife he was holding and went to the window to rearrange the tray of lamb chops that Frank had just put there. 'Haven't you any idea how to put meat on a tray to make it look attractive?'

'I was trying to be quick.'

'You can't hurry a job like this. That's why Percy starts so early. He's an artist in his way. His windows are a picture. I wonder what's happened to him.'

'He could be dead.'

Joe turned to look at Frank with clear disfavour. 'That's a very unpleasant suggestion.'

'It's a possibility. He's always falling off that old bike. Well, he could have been taken to hospital, anyway.'

'Someone would have phoned by now.'

'All right, perhaps he died in the night,' persisted Frank. 'He could be lying in his bed. He lives alone, doesn't he?'

'You're talking nonsense, lad.'

'Can you think of anything better?'

'Any more lip from you, young man, and I'll see that you get your cards. Get the chickens out. I'll attend to this.'

'Do you mean the frozen birds, Mr Wilkins?'

'The farm birds. I'll tell you if we need any frozen in a minute or two.'

'Do you think we ought to phone the hospital, Mr Wilkins, just in case something has happened to Percy?'

'What good would that do?'

Frank took seven capons from the chiller and hung them on the rail above the window. 'That's all there is,' he told Joe. 'Shall I get out some frozen ones?'

Joe shook his head. 'It's Monday, isn't it? There isn't much call for poultry on a Monday.'

'We'll need them for tomorrow. They need to thaw. We won't be getting any farm birds this week with Mr Pugh on holiday.'

Joe hesitated in his rearrangement of the window display. 'You've got a point there, lad.'

Frank waited.

'Yes,' said Joe. 'We shall want some frozen birds.'

'Have you got the key?'

'The key?'

'There's a padlock on the freezer door.'

Joe crossed the shop to take a look. It was a heavy padlock. It secured the hasp on the freezer door over an iron staple. He said, 'Silly old beggar. What does he want to lock it for?'

'There's a lot of meat in there,' said Frank, in Percy's defence. 'Have you got the key?'

Joe shook his head. 'I reckon he takes it home with him.'

Frank swore. 'What are we going to do? We've got to get in there. It's not just the chickens. It's the New Zealand. We're right down on lamb.'

'We'd better look for the key, just in case he leaves it somewhere,' said Joe, opening one of the drawers under the counter.

Their short search did not turn up the key.

'I think I could force it with that old file of yours,' suggested Frank.

'No, lad, you might damage the door. You don't want to get your marching orders from Mr Pugh. I've got one of those small hacksaws in my toolbag in the car. We'll use that to cut through the padlock.'

A short time later he returned with the saw. He held the padlock firm while Frank started sawing through the staple.

'All this trouble because of Percy,' said Frank. 'I'd like to strangle the old git.'

'It might not be his fault after all,' said Joe. 'Mr Pugh might have given him orders to use a padlock. He's dead scared of the boss. He does exactly what he's told, and I don't blame him. I heard Mr Pugh laying into him on Saturday night after you left to deliver those orders. It was vicious, it really was.'

Frank continued sawing. 'What was it about?'

'Well, you were there when Mr Pugh walked in out of nowhere, saying he wanted to see that things were straight before he went off for his week in Majorca. That was before you left with the orders.'

'Yes, he'd just picked up his tickets from the travel agent.'

'Right. You'd think he'd be on top of the world, wouldn't you, just about to push off for a week in the sun? Not Mr Pugh. He happened to catch old Percy putting away the cuts we hadn't sold.'

'There's nothing wrong with that, is there?'

'No, but Percy left the door of the chiller open while he was doing it. We all do it, but Percy got caught. You should have heard Mr Pugh go for him, ranting and raving about the cost of running a cold chamber with employees who are so idle that they let the cold air out when they can't be bothered to open and close the door a few times. He really laid it on thick. He was quoting things about cubic feet of air and thermal units as if old Percy had done it deliberately.'

'Almost there,' said Frank. 'Mind it doesn't catch your hand.'

The hacksaw blade cut cleanly through the staple.

Joe said, 'Good.' But he was determined to finish his story. 'He told Percy he was too old for the job and he ought to retire soon. Percy started pleading with him. I tell you, Frank, I was so embarrassed that I didn't want to hear any more. I left them to it and went home.'

'I'll get out those frozen birds,' said Frank as he slipped the padlock from the hasp.

'You'd have a job to find a meaner man than Mr Pugh,' Joe continued as Frank swung back the door of the freezer chamber. 'Going on like that at an old man who's worked here all his life – and all for the sake of a few pence more on his electricity bill, when we all know he makes enough profit to have holidays in Spain. What's the matter, lad?'

Frank had uttered a strange cry as he entered the chamber.

Joe looked in and saw him standing over the huddled, hoar-white figure of a dead man. He went closer and crouched to look at the face. It was glistening with a patina of frost.

It was the face of Mr Pugh.

Joe placed his hand on Frank's shoulder and said, 'Come away, lad. There's nothing we can do.'

From somewhere Joe produced a hipflask and poured some scotch for Frank as they sat in the shop and stared at the door of the freezer.

'We'll have to call the police,' said Frank.

'I'll do it presently.'

'He must have been trapped in there all the week-end.'

'He wouldn't have known much about it,' said Joe. 'He must have died inside a few hours.'

'How could it have happened?'

Joe stared into space and said nothing.

'There's a handle on the inside of that door,' said Frank, speaking his thoughts as they rushed through the implications. 'Anyone caught in there can open the door and walk out, usually. But he couldn't get out because the padlock was on the outside. Someone must have put it there. It must have been Percy. Why, Mr Wilkins, why would Percy do a thing like that?'

Joe gave a shrug and still kept silent.

Frank supplied his own answer: 'He must have panicked when he thought he would lose his job. He'd been in fear of losing it for years. He found some way of persuading Mr Pugh to go into the freeze chamber, and then he locked him inside. I know what he did. He told Mr Pugh the handle on the inside was too stiff to move, and he liked to leave the door open because he was scared of being trapped. Mr Pugh said he was making excuses and stepped inside to show how easy it was to get out.' Frank began to smile. 'Mr Wilkins, I think I'm going to laugh.'

The tension relaxed a little.

'I'll tell you something funnier than that,' said Joe. 'Why do you think Percy hasn't come in this morning?'

'Well, it's obvious. He knew we'd open that door and find the body.'

'Yes, but where do you think he is?'

Frank frowned and shook his head. 'At home?'

Joe grinned and said, 'Majorca.'

'No!' Frank rocked with laughter. 'The crafty old beggar!'

'When Mr Pugh came in on Saturday, he had a large brown envelope with him containing his travel tickets.'

'I remember. I saw it. He put it on the counter by the cash register.'

'Well, it isn't there now, is it?'

Frank said, 'You can't help admiring him. He's probably sitting on the hotel terrace at this minute ordering his breakfast and thinking of you and me finding Mr Pugh in the freezer.'

'I'd better phone the police,' said Joe, getting up.

'You know, if it wasn't for that padlock on the door, no one would suspect what happened,' said Frank. 'Mr Pugh might have just felt ill and fainted in there. They'd call it misadventure, or something.'

'And Percy would get away with it,' said Joe reflectively. 'It isn't as if he's a vicious murderer. He's no danger to anyone else.'

'I could get rid of it,' offered Frank. 'I could put it in the pannier on my bike and get rid of it lunchtime.'

'We'd have to stick to the same story,' said Joe. 'We just opened the door and found him lying there.'

'It's the truth,' said Frank. 'We don't need to say a word about the padlock. Shall we do it? Poor old Percy – he hasn't had many breaks.'

'All right,' confirmed Joe. 'We'll do it.'

After they had shaken hands, he picked up the phone and called the police. Frank took the padlock to his

153

motorbike in the yard at the back of the shop, and secreted it under the toolbag in the pannier.

A squad car drew up outside the shop within five minutes of Joe's call. A bearded sergeant and a constable came in and Joe opened the freeze chamber and showed them Mr Pugh's body. Frank described how he had found the body. He omitted to mention the padlock. Joe confirmed Frank's statement.

'So it looks as if the body's been lying in there since you closed on Saturday,' said the sergeant after they had withdrawn to the warmer air of the shop. 'You say that Mr Pugh looked in late in the afternoon. What did he want?'

'He was just making sure that everything was in order before he went on holiday,' said Joe.

'He was off to Majorca for a week,' added Frank.

'Lucky man,' put in the constable.

The sergeant gave him a withering look. 'Was Mr Pugh in good health?' he asked Joe.

'I thought he looked rather off-colour,' answered Joe. 'He drove himself hard, you know.'

'He needed that holiday,' said Frank, quick to see the point of what Joe was suggesting.

'Well, he didn't get it,' said the sergeant. 'He must have collapsed. Heart, I expect. The doctor will tell us. There's an ambulance on the way. I suggest you keep the shop closed for a couple of hours. I shall want statements from both of you. Was there anyone else working here on Saturday?'

'Only Percy – Mr Maddox,' answered Joe. 'He isn't in this morning. I believe he was going to ask Mr Pugh for a few days off.'

'I see. We'll want a statement from him. Have you got his address?'

'He told me he was hoping to go away,' said Joe.

'We'll catch up with him later, then. Which of you was the last to leave on Saturday?'

'That was Percy,' said Joe.

'He stays behind to clear up,' explained Frank.

'He puts things away, you mean?' said the sergeant.

'That's right,' said Joe. 'He's getting on a bit, you know. Worked here for years. A bit slow now, but he likes to be useful. He puts everything away at the end of the day.'

'In the freezer?'

Joe shook his head. 'We don't re-freeze meat. It has to be put in the chiller at the end of the day.'

'So he wouldn't have opened the freezer door?'

'It's very unlikely,' said Joe. 'If he had, he'd have found Mr Pugh, wouldn't he?'

They took a statement from Frank. He said nothing to incriminate Percy. He simply explained how he had seen Mr Pugh come into the shop late on Saturday afternoon, shortly before he (Frank) had left to deliver the orders. As for this morning, he had opened the freezer door and found Mr Pugh dead on the floor. The constable read the statement back and Frank signed it. 'Would you like some coffee and a fresh doughnut?' he asked the policemen. 'We always have a doughnut in the morning. It's my job to collect them from Jonquil's. I go on my bike, and they're still warm when I get back.'

'I like the sound of that,' said the sergeant, putting his hand in his pocket. 'How much are they?'

Frank felt an exhilarating sense of release as he wheeled his motorcycle into the street and started the engine. He rode up the hill towards the baker's, stopping a few yards short, by the place where the front of the delicatessen was being renovated. Outside was a builder's skip containing old wood and masonry. Frank took the padlock from his pannier and dropped it unobtrusively into the skip. He collected the bag of doughnuts from the baker's and drove back to the shop.

An ambulance had drawn up outside. As Frank approached, one of the attendants was closing the rear door. The man walked round the side of the vehicle and got in. It moved away. The few bystanders who had collected outside the shop moved on.

When Frank went in, Joe had already made the coffee. He was talking to the police about football.

'We should have gone by now,' the sergeant told Frank. 'We've got both your statements and the body's been collected, but we didn't want to miss those doughnuts.'

Frank handed them around.

'Still warm,' said the sergeant. 'I hope you observed the speed limit, lad.'

Frank smiled.

The police finished their coffee and doughnuts and left the shop.

Frank heaved a huge breath of relief.

Joe took out his handkerchief and mopped his forehead. 'Did you get rid of it?'

Frank nodded.

'Well done,' said Joe. 'Well done, Frank.'

'I reckon old Percy owes us both a beer after that,' said Frank.

'It was worth more than that,' said Joe.

'We couldn't have turned him in,' said Frank.

They opened the shop. Customers who had seen the shop closed earlier now returned in force. They all wanted to know what the police had been doing there and whether it was a body that the ambulancemen had collected. Joe and Frank explained that they were unable to comment. The enquiries persisted and the queue got longer.

'If you ask me,' one woman notorious for voicing her opinions said, 'it was that old boy who sweeps the floor. He was far too old to be working in a shop.'

'If you mean Percy Maddox, you're wrong,' said the woman next in line. 'There's nothing wrong with Percy. He's coming up the street on his bike.'

Joe dropped the cleaver he was using and went to the window. He was joined by Frank, who gave a long, low whistle of amazement.

'Crazy old man!' said Joe angrily. 'What does he think he's up to? He ought to be in Spain.'

They watched through the window as Percy came to a halt outside the shop, dismounted, removed his cycle clips and wheeled his bicycle up the side passage. A moment later he appeared in the shop, a slight, bald-headed, worried-looking man in a faded grey suit. He picked his apron off the hook and started getting into it. 'Morning, ladies,' he said to the queue, then turned to Joe and said, 'Morning, Joe. Shall I tidy up the window? It's a bit of mess.'

Joe said, 'What are you doing, coming in here?'

'Sorry I'm late,' said Percy. 'The police kept me waiting.'

'You've been to the police?' said Joe in a shrill voice. 'What did you tell them?'

Frank said, 'Listen, I've just thought of something. I'd better go and fetch it.' He started untying his apron.

But he was slower than Joe, who was already out of his. He said, 'You stay. I'll go.'

While Frank was saying, 'But you don't know where I put it,' Joe was round the corner and out to the street.

He didn't get far. Apparently from nowhere, two

policemen grabbed him. A squad car drew up and he was bundled into the back. It drove away, its blue light flashing.

'Who's next?' said Percy, who had taken Joe's place at the counter.

An hour or so later, when there was no queue left and Frank and Percy had the shop to themselves, Frank said, 'What's going to happen to Joe?'

'Plenty of questions, I should think,' answered Percy. 'You know about Mr Pugh being found dead, don't you?'

'I was the one who found him.'

'Well, Joe must have murdered him.'

'Joe? We thought it was you.'

Percy blinked. 'Me, son?'

'When you didn't come in this morning, we thought you must have bunked off to Spain with that ticket Mr Pugh left on the counter.'

'But why should I want to kill Mr Pugh after all these years?'

'Well, because of the bad time he gives you, all those long hours without a word of thanks. Exploitation, Joe called it.'

'Did he, by George?' said Percy with a smile.

'He said there was a bit of a scene on Saturday because you left the freezer door open. He said he felt so embarrassed that he cleared off home while Mr Pugh was still laying into you.'

Percy shook his head. 'Son, that isn't true. I left before Joe on Friday. Mr Pugh had told me it might be better if I wasn't around while he did some stocktaking with Joe. We had our suspicions about Joe, you see. The books weren't right. There were big discrepancies. Mr Pugh and I decided to check things carefully for a week and confront Joe with the evidence on Saturday after we closed.'

Frank's eyes widened. 'Mr Pugh and *you*?'

'Yes, you weren't to know this, and nor was Joe, but Mr Pugh made me a partner last year, after I'd done fifty years in the shop. Nice of him, wasn't it? I told him I wouldn't ever make a manager, and I certainly didn't want to upset Joe, so we agreed to keep the partnership a secret, just between Mr Pugh and me, and I carried on the same as ever, with the work I know best. But as things have turned out, with me the surviving partner, I can't keep it a secret any longer, can I? It's my shop now. I'm the boss.'

Frank was shaking his head, trying to understand. 'So did you put the police on to Joe?'

Percy nodded. 'But I didn't mean to. I didn't know what had happened. On Sunday morning Joe drove over to see me. He told me Mr Pugh had changed his mind about going to Spain because the auditors were coming to look at the books. He had asked Joe to offer the ticket to me. I believed him. I thought he wanted me out of the way to spare me any unpleasantness.'

'When it was really Joe who wanted you out of the way,' said Frank. He recollected the events of the morning, the way Joe had tricked him into covering up the crime out of sympathy for Percy, when in reality Percy was innocent. The trick had almost succeeded too. The police had gone away convinced that Mr Pugh had died by misadventure. They had not suspected murder, and they certainly had not suspected Joe of committing it. But now he was under arrest. 'Well, if you weren't suspicious of Joe,' Frank said to Percy, 'why aren't you in Spain? What made you go to the police?'

Percy picked up Joe's straw boater. 'You know how it is with me, son. I haven't had a holiday in years, let alone a holiday abroad. I haven't got a passport. I dropped in at the police station to ask where I can get one, and...' He handed the boater to Frank. 'I need a new manager now, don't I?'

You Can't Be Too Careful

Ruth Rendell

Ruth Rendell

You Can't Be Too Careful

Della Galway went out with a man for the first (and almost the last) time on her nineteenth birthday. He parked his car, and as they were going into the restaurant she asked him if he had locked all the doors and the boot. When he turned back and said, yes, he'd better do that, she asked him why he didn't have a burglar-proof locking device on the steering wheel.

Her parents had brought her up to be cautious. When she left that happy home in that safe little provincial town, she took her parents' notions with her to London. At first she could only afford the rent of a single room. It upset her that the other tenants often came in late at night and left the front door on the latch. Although her room was at the top of the house and she had nothing worth stealing, she lay in bed sweating with fear. At work it was just the same. Nobody bothered about security measures. Della was always the last to leave, and sometimes she went back two or three times to check that all the office doors and the outer door were shut.

The personnel officer suggested she see a psychiatrist.

Della was very ambitious. She had an economics degree, a business studies diploma, and had come out top at the end of her secretarial course. She knew a psychiatrist would find something wrong with her – they had to earn their money like everyone else – and long sessions of treatment would follow which wouldn't help her towards her goal, that of becoming the company's first woman director. They always held that sort of thing against you.

'That won't be necessary,' she said in her brisk way. 'It was the firm's property I was worried about. If they like to risk losing their valuable equipment, that's their look-out.'

She stopped going back to check the doors – it didn't prey on her mind much as her own safety wasn't involved – and three weeks later two men broke in, stole all the electric typewriters and damaged the computer beyond repair. It proved her right, but she didn't say so. The threat of the psychiatrist had frightened her so much that she never again aired her burglar obsession at work.

When she got promotion and a salary rise, she decided to get a flat of her own. The landlady was a woman after her own heart. Mrs Swanson liked Della from the first and explained to her, as to a kindred spirit, the security arrangements.

'This is a very nice neighbourhood, Miss Galway, but the crime rate in London is rising all the time, and I always say you can't be too careful.'

Della said she couldn't agree more.

'So I always keep this side gate bolted on the inside. The back door into this little yard must also be kept locked and bolted. The bathroom window looks out into the garden, you see, so I like the garden door and the bathroom door to be locked at night too.'

'Very wise,' said Della, noting that the window in the bed-sitting room had screws fixed to its sashes which prevented its being opened more than six inches. 'What did you say the rent was?'

'Twenty pounds a week.' Mrs Swanson was a landlady first, and a kindred spirit secondly, so when Della hesitated, she said, 'It's a garden flat, completely self-contained and you've got your own phone. I shan't have any trouble in letting it. I've got someone else coming to view it at two.'

Della stopped hesitating. She moved in at the end of the week, having supplied Mrs Swanson with references and assured her she was quiet, prudent as to locks and bolts, and not inclined to have 'unauthorised' people to stay overnight. By unauthorised people Mrs Swanson meant men. Since the episode over the car on her nineteenth birthday, Della had entered tentatively upon friendships with men, but no man had ever taken her out more than twice and none had ever got as far as to kiss her. She didn't know why this was, as she had always been polite and pleasant, insisting on paying her share, careful to carry her own coat, handbag and parcels so as to give her escort no trouble, ever watchful of his wallet and keys, offering to have the theatre tickets in her own safe keeping, and anxious not to keep him out too late. That one after another men dropped her worried her very little. No spark of sexual feeling had ever troubled her, and the idea of sharing her orderly, routine-driven life with a man – untidy, feckless, casual creatures as they all, with the exception of her father, seemed to be – was a daunting one. She meant to get to the top on her own. One day perhaps, when she was about thirty-five and with a high-powered lady executive's salary, then if some like-minded, quiet and prudent man came along... In the meantime, Mrs Swanson had no need to worry.

Della was very happy with her flat. It was utterly quiet, a little sanctum tucked at the back of the house. She never heard a sound from her neighbours in the other parts of the house and they, of course, never heard a sound from her. She encountered them occasionally when crossing from her own front door to the front door of the house. They were mouselike people who scuttled off to their holes with no more than a nod and a 'good evening.' This was as it should be. The flat, too, was entirely as it should be.

The bed-sitter looked just like a living-room by day, for the bed was let down from a curtained recess in the wall only at night. Its window overlooked the yard which Della never used. She never unbolted the side gate or the back door or, needless to say, attempted to undo the screws and open the window more than six inches.

Every evening, when she had washed the dishes and wiped down every surface in the immaculate well-fitted kitchen, had her bath, made her bedtime drink, and let the bed down from the wall, she went on her security rounds just as her father did at home. First she unlocked and unbolted the back door and crossed the yard to check that the side gate was securely fastened. It always was as no one ever touched it, but Della liked to make absolutely sure, and sometimes went back several times in case her eyes had deceived her. Then she bolted and locked the back door, the garden door and the bathroom door. All these doors opened out of a small room, about ten feet square – Mrs Swanson called it the garden room – which in its turn could be locked off by yet another door from the kitchen. Della locked it. She rather regretted she couldn't lock the door that led from the kitchen into the bed-sitting room but, owing to some oversight on Mrs Swanson's part, there was no lock on it. However, her own front door in the bed-sitter itself was locked, of course, on the Yale. Finally, before getting into bed, she bolted the front door.

Then she was safe. Though she sometimes got up once or twice more to make assurance trebly sure, she generally settled down at this point into blissful sleep, certain that even the most accomplished of burglars couldn't break in.

There was only one drawback – the rent.

'That flat,' said Mrs Swanson, 'is really intended for two people. A married couple had it before you, and before that two ladies shared it.'

'I couldn't share my bed,' said Della with a shudder, 'or, come to that, my room.'

'If you found a nice friend to share I wouldn't object to putting up a single bed in the garden room. Then your friend could come and go by the side gate, provided you were prepared to *promise* me it would always be bolted at night.'

Della wasn't going to advertise for a flatmate. You couldn't be too careful. Yet she had to find someone if she was going to afford any new winter clothes, not to mention heating the place. It would have to be the right person, someone to fill all her own exacting requirements as well as satisfy Mrs Swanson...

'Ooh, it's lovely!' said Rosamund Vine. 'It's so quiet and clean. And you've got a garden! You should see the dump I've been living in. It was over-run with mice.'

'You don't get mice,' said Della repressively, 'unless you leave food about.'

'I won't do that. I'll be ever so careful. I'll go halves with the rent and I'll have the key to the back door, shall I? That way I won't disturb you if I come in late at night.'

'I hope you won't come in late at night,' said Della. 'Mrs Swanson's very particular about that sort of thing.'

'Don't worry.' Rosamund sounded rather bitter. 'I've nothing and no one to keep me out late. Anyway, the last bus passes the end of the road at a quarter to twelve.'

Della pushed aside her misgivings, and Mrs Swanson, interviewing Rosamund, appeared to have none. She made a point of explaining the safety precautions, to which Rosamund listened meekly and with earnest nods of her head. Della was glad this duty hadn't fallen to her, as she didn't want Rosamund to tell exaggerated tales about her at work. So much the better if she could put it all on Mrs Swanson.

Rosamund Vine had been chosen with the care Della devoted to every choice she made. It had taken three weeks of observation and keeping her ears open to select her. It wouldn't do to find someone on too low a salary or, on the other hand, someone with too lofty a position in the company. She didn't like the idea of a spectacularly good-looking girl, for such led hectic lives, or too clever a girl, for such might involve her in tiresome arguments. An elegant girl would fill the cupboards with clothes and the bathroom with cosmetics. A gifted girl would bring in musical instruments or looms or paints or trunks full of books. Only Rosamund, of all the candidates, qualified. She was small and quiet and prettyish, a secretary (though not Della's secretary), the daughter of a clergyman who, by coincidence, had been at the same university at the same time as Della's father. Della, who had much the same attitude as Victorian employers had to their maids' 'followers', noted that she had never heard her speak of a boy friend or overheard any cloakroom gossip as to Rosamund's love life.

The two girls settled down happily together. They seldom went out in the evenings. Della always went to bed at eleven sharp and would have relegated

Rosamund to her own room at this point but for one small difficulty. With Rosamund in the garden room – necessarily sitting on her bed as there was nowhere else to sit – it wasn't possible for Della to make her security rounds. Only once had she tried doing it with Rosamund looking on.

'Goodness,' Rosamund had said, 'this place is like Fort Knox. All those keys and bolts! What are you so scared of?'

'Mrs Swanson likes to have the place locked up,' said Della, but the next night she made hot drinks for the two of them and sent Rosamund to wait for her in the bed-sitter before creeping out into the yard for a secret check-up.

When she came back Rosamund was examining her bedside table. 'Why do you put everything in order like that, Della? Your book at right angles to the table and your cigarette packet at right angles to your book, and, look, your ashtray's exactly an inch from the lamp as if you'd measured it out.'

'Because I'm a naturally tidy person.'

'I do think it's funny your smoking. I never would have guessed you smoked till I came to live here. It doesn't sort of seem in character. And your glass of water. Do you want to drink water in the night?'

'Not always,' Della said patiently. 'But I might want to, and I shouldn't want to have to get up and fetch it, should I?'

Rosamund's questions didn't displease her. It showed that the girl wanted to learn the right way to do things. Della taught her that a room must be dusted every day, the fridge de-frosted once a week, the table laid for breakfast before they went to bed, all the windows closed and the catches fastened. She drew Rosamund out as to the places she had previously lived in with a view to contrasting past squalor with present comfort, and she received a shock when Rosamund made it plain that in some of those rooms, attics, converted garages, she had lived with a man. Della made no comment but froze slightly. And Rosamund, thank goodness, seemed to understand her disapproval and didn't go into details. But soon after that she began going out in the evenings.

Della didn't want to know where she was going or with whom. She had plenty to occupy her own evenings, what with the work she brought home, her housework, washing and ironing, her twice-weekly letter to her mother and father, and the commercial Spanish she was teaching herself from gramophone records. It was rather a relief not to have Rosamund fluttering about. Besides, she could do her security rounds in peace. Not, of course, that she could check up on the side gate till Rosamund came in. Necessarily, it had to remain unbolted, and the back door to which Rosamund had the key, unlocked. But always by ten to twelve at the latest she'd hear the side gate open and close and hear Rosamund pause to draw the bolts. Then her feet tiptoeing across the yard, then the back door unlocked, shut, locked. After that, Della could sleep in peace.

The first problem arose when Rosamund came in one night and didn't bolt the gate after her. Della listened carefully in the dark, but she was positive those bolts had not been drawn. Even if the back door was locked, it was unthinkable to leave that side gate on nothing all night but its flimsy latch. She put on her dressing gown and went through the kitchen into the garden room. Rosamund was already in bed, her clothes flung about on the coverlet. Della picked them up and folded them. She was coming back from the yard, having fastened those bolts, when Rosamund sat up and said:

169

'What's the matter? Can't you sleep?'

'Mrs Swanson,' said Della with a light indulgent laugh, 'wouldn't be able to sleep if she knew you'd left that side gate unbolted.'

'Did I? Honestly, Della, I don't know what I'm doing half the time. I can't think of anyone but Chris. He's the most marvellous person and I do think he's just as mad about me as I am about him. I feel as if he's changed my whole life.'

Della let her spend nearly all the following evening describing the marvellous Chris, how brilliant he was – though at present unable to get a job fitting his talents – how amusing, how highly educated – though so poor as to be reduced to borrowing a friend's room while that friend was away. She listened and smiled and made appropriate remarks, but she wondered when she had last been so bored. Every time she got up to try and play one of her Spanish records, Rosamund was off again on another facet of Chris's dazzling personality, until at last Della had to say she had a headache and would Rosamund mind leaving her on her own for a bit?

'Anyway, you'll see him tomorrow. I've asked him for a meal.'

Unluckily, this happened to be the evening Della was going to supper with her aunt on the other side of London. They had evidently enjoyed themselves, judging by the mess in the kitchen, Della thought when she got home. There were few things she disliked more than wet dishes left to drain. Rosamund was asleep. Della crept out into the yard and checked that the bolts were fastened.

'I heard you wandering about ever so late,' said Rosamund in the morning. 'Were you upset about anything?'

'Certainly not. I simply found it rather hard to get to sleep because it was past my normal time.'

'Aren't you funny?' said Rosamund, and she giggled.

The next night she missed the last bus.

Della had passed a pleasant evening, studying firstly the firm's annual report, then doing a Spanish exercise. By eleven she was in bed, reading the memoirs of a woman company chairman. Her bedside light went off at half-past and she lay in the dark waiting for the sound of the side gate.

Her clock had luminous hands, and when they passed ten to twelve she began to feel a nasty tingly jumping sensation all over her body. She put on the light, switched it off immediately. She didn't want Rosamund bursting in with all her silly questions and comments. But Rosamund didn't burst in, and the hands of the clock closed together on midnight. There was no doubt about it. The last bus had gone and Rosamund hadn't been on it.

Well, the silly girl needn't think she was going to stand this sort of thing. She'd bolt that side gate herself and Rosamund could stay out in the street all night. Of course she might ring the front door bell, she was silly and inconsiderate enough to do that, but it couldn't be helped. Della would far rather be awakened at one or two o'clock than lie there knowing that side gate was open for anyone to come in. She put on her dressing gown and made her way through the spotless kitchen to the garden room. Rosamund had hung a silly sort of curtain over the back door, not a curtain really but a rather dirty Indian bedspread. Della lifted it distastefully – and then she realised. She couldn't bolt the side gate because the back door into the yard was locked and Rosamund had the key.

A practical person like herself wasn't going to be

done that way. She'd go out by the front door, walk round to the side entrance and – but, no, that wouldn't work either. If she opened the gate and bolted it on the inside, she'd simply find herself bolted inside the yard. The only thing was to climb out of the window. She tried desperately to undo the window screws, but they had seized up from years of disuse and she couldn't shift them. Trembling now, she sat down on the edge of her bed and lit a cigarette. For the first time in her life she was in an insecure place by night, alone in a London flat, with nothing to separate her from hordes of rapacious burglars but a feeble back door lock which any type of a thief could pick open in five minutes.

How criminally careless of Mrs Swanson not to have provided the door between the bed-sitter and the kitchen with a lock! There was no heavy piece of furniture she could place against the door. The phone was by her bed, of course. But if she heard a sound and dialled for the police was there a chance of their getting there before she was murdered and the place ransacked?

What Mrs Swanson had provided was one of the most fearsome-looking breadknives Della had ever seen. She fetched it from the kitchen and put it under her pillow. Its presence made her feel slightly safer, but suppose she didn't wake up when the man came in, suppose...? That was ridiculous, she wouldn't sleep at all. Exhausted, shaken, feeling physically sick, she crawled under the bedclothes and, after concentrated thought, put the light out. Perhaps, if there was no light on, he would go past her, not know she was there, make his way into the main part of the house, and if by then she hadn't actually died of fright...

At twenty minutes past one, when she had reached the point of deciding to phone for a car to take her to an hotel, the side gate clicked and Rosamund entered the yard. Della fell back against the pillows with a relief so tremendous that she couldn't even bother to go out and check the bolts. So what if it wasn't bolted? The man would have to pass Rosamund first, kill her first. Della found she didn't care at all about what might happen to Rosamund, only about her own safety.

She sneaked out at half-past six to put the knife back, and she was sullenly eating her breakfast, the flat immaculate, when Rosamund appeared at eight.

'I missed the last bus. I had to get a taxi.'

'You could have phoned.'

'Goodness, you sound just like my mother. It was bad enough having to get up and...' Rosamund blushed and put her hand over her mouth. 'I mean, go *out* and get that taxi and...Well, I wasn't all that late,' she muttered.

Her little slip of the tongue hadn't been lost on Della. But she was too tired to make any rejoinder beyond saying that Mrs Swanson would be very annoyed if she knew, and would Rosamund give her fair warning next time she intended to be late? Rosamund said when they met again that evening that she couldn't give her fair warning, as she could never be sure herself. Della said no more. What, anyway, would be the use of knowing what time Rosamund was coming in when she couldn't bolt the gate?

Three mornings later her temper flared.

On two of the intervening nights Rosamund had missed the last bus. The funny thing was that she didn't look at all tired or jaded, while Della was worn-out. For three hours on the previous night she had lain stiffly clutching the breadknife while the old house creaked about her and the side gate rattled in the wind.

'I don't know why you bother to come home at all.'

'Won't you mind if I don't?'

'Not a bit. Do as you like.'

Stealthily, before Rosamund left the flat by the front door, Della slipped out and bolted the gate. Rosamund, of course (being utterly imprudent), didn't check the gate before she locked the back door. Della fell into a heavy sleep at ten o'clock to be awakened just after two by a thudding on the side gate followed by a frenzied ringing of the front door bell.

'You locked me out!' Rosamund sobbed. 'Even my mother never did that. I was locked out in the street and I'm frozen. What have I done to you that you treat me like that?'

'You said you weren't coming home.'

'I wasn't going to, but we went out and Chris forgot his key. He's had to sleep at a friend's place. I wish I'd gone there too!'

They were evidently two of a kind. Well-suited, Della thought. Although it was nearly half-past two in the morning, this seemed the best moment to have things out. She addressed Rosamund in her precise schoolmistressy voice.

'I think we'll have to make other arrangements, Rosamund. Your ways aren't my ways, and we don't really get on, do we? You can stay here till you find somewhere else, but I'd like you to start looking round straightaway.'

'But what have I *done*? I haven't made a noise or had my friends here. I haven't even used your phone, not once. Honestly, Della, I've done my best to keep the place clean and tidy, and it's nearly killed me.'

'I've explained what I mean. We're not the same kind of people.'

'I'll go on Saturday. I'll go to my mother – it won't be any worse. God knows – and then maybe Chris and I...'

'You'd better go to bed now,' Della said coldly, but she couldn't get any sleep herself. She was wondering how she had been such a bad judge of character, and wondering too what she was going to do about the rent. Find someone else, of course. An older woman perhaps, a widow or a middle-aged spinster...

What she was determined not to do was reveal to Rosamund, at this late stage, her anxiety about the side gate. If anything remained to comfort her, it was the knowledge that Rosamund thought her strong, mature and sensible. But not revealing it brought her an almost unbearable agony. For Rosamund seemed to think the very sight of her would be an embarrassment to Della. Each evening she was gone from the flat before Della got home, and each time she had gone out leaving the side gate unbolted and the back door locked. Della had no way of knowing whether she would come in on the last bus or get a taxi or be seen home in the small hours by Chris. She didn't know whether Chris lived near or far away, and now she wished she had listened more closely to Rosamund's confidences and asked a few questions of her own. Instead, she had only thought with a shudder how nasty it must be to have to sleep with a man, and had wondered if she would ever bring herself to face the prospect.

Each night she took the breadknife to bed with her, confirmed in her conviction that she wasn't being unreasonable when one of the mouselike people whom she met in the hall told her the house next door had been broken into and its old woman occupant knocked on the head. Rosamund came in once at one, once at half-past two, and once she didn't come in at all. Della got great bags under her eyes and her skin looked grey. She fell asleep over her desk at work, while a bright-eyed vivacious Rosamund regaled her friends in the cloakroom about the joys of her relationship with Chris.

But now there was only one more night to go...

Rosamund had left a note to say she wouldn't be home. She'd see Della on the following evening when she collected her cases to take them to her mother. But she'd left the side gate unbolted. Della seriously considered bolting it and then climbing back over it into the side entrance, but it was too high and smooth for her to climb and there wasn't a ladder. Nothing for it but to begin her vigil with the cigarettes, the glass of water, the phone and the breadknife. It ought to have been easier, this last night, just because it was the last. Instead it was worse than any of the others. She lay in the dark, thinking of the old woman next door, of the house that was precisely the same as the one next door, and of the intruder who now knew the best and simplest way in. She tried to think of something else, anything else, but the strongest instinct of all over-rode all her feeble attempts to concentrate on tomorrow, on work, on ambition, on the freedom and peace of tomorrow when that gate would be fastened for good, never again to be opened.

Rosamund had said she wouldn't be in. But you couldn't rely on a word she said. Della wasn't, therefore, surprised (though she was overwhelmingly relieved) to hear the gate click just before two. Sighing with a kind of ecstasy – for tomorrow had come – she listened for the sound of the bolts being drawn across. The sound didn't come. Well, that was a small thing. She'd fasten the bolts herself when Rosamund was in bed. She heard footsteps moving very softly, and then the back door was unlocked. Rosamund took a longer time than usual about unlocking it, but maybe she was tired or drunk or heaven knew what.

Silence.

Then the back door creaked and made rattling sounds as if Rosamund hadn't bothered to re-lock it. Wearily, Della hoisted herself out of bed and slipped her dressing gown round her. As she did so, the kitchen light came on. The light showed round the edges of the old door in a brilliant phosphorescent rectangle. That wasn't like Rosamund who never went into the kitchen, who fell immediately into bed without even bothering to wash her face. A long shiver ran through Della. Her body taut but trembling, she listened. Footsteps were crossing the kitchen floor and the fridge door was opened. She heard the sounds of fumbling in cupboards, a drawer was opened and silver rattled. She wanted to call out, 'Rosamund, Rosamund, is that you?' but she had no voice. Her mouth was dry and her voice had gone. Something occurred to her that had never struck her before. It struck her with a great thrust of terror. How would she know, how had she ever known, whether it was Rosamund or another who entered the flat by the side gate and the frail back door?

Then there came a cough.

It was a slight cough, the sound of someone clearing his throat, but it was unmistakably *his* throat. There was a man in the kitchen.

Della forgot the phone. She remembered – though she had scarcely for a moment forgotten her – the old woman next door. Blind terror thrust her to her feet, plunged her hand under the pillow for the knife. She opened the kitchen door, and he was there, a tall man, young and strong, standing right there on the threshold with Mrs Swanson's silver in one hand and Mrs Swanson's heavy iron pan in the other. Della didn't hesitate. She struck hard with the knife, struck again and again until the bright blood flew across the white walls and the clean ironing and the table neatly laid for breakfast.

The policeman was very nice to Rosamund Vine. He called her by her Christian name and gave her a cup of coffee. She drank the coffee, though she didn't really want it as she had had a cup at the hospital when they told her Chris was dead.

'Tell me about last night, will you, Rosamund?'

'I'd been out with my boy friend – Chris – Chris Maitland. He'd forgotten his key and he hadn't anywhere to sleep, so I said to come back with me. He was going to leave early in the morning before she – before Della was up. We were going to be very careful about that. And we were terribly quiet. We crept in at about two.'

'You didn't call out?'

'No, we thought she was asleep. That's why we didn't speak to each other, not even in whispers. But she must have heard us.' Her voice broke a little. 'I went straight to bed. Chris was hungry. I said if he was as quiet as a mouse he could get himself something from the fridge, and I told him where the knives and forks and plates were. The next thing I heard this ghastly scream and I ran out and – and Chris was ... There was blood everywhere ...'

The policeman waited until she was calmer.

'Why do you think she attacked him with a knife?' he asked.

'I don't know.'

'I think you do, Rosamund.'

'Perhaps I do.' Rosamund looked down. 'She didn't like me going out.'

'Because she was afraid of being there alone?'

'Della Galway,' said Rosamund, 'wasn't afraid of anything. Mrs Swanson was nervous about burglars, but Della wasn't. Everyone in the house knew about the woman next door getting coshed, and they were all nervous. Except Della. She didn't even mention it to me, and she must have known.'

'So she didn't think Chris was a burglar?'

'Of course she didn't.' Rosamund started to cry. 'She saw a man – my man. She couldn't get one of her own. Every time I tried to talk about him she went all cold and stand-offish. She heard us come in last night and she understood and – and it sent her over the edge. It drove her crazy. I'd heard they wanted her to see a psychiatrist at work, and now I know why.'

The policeman shivered a little in spite of his long experience. Fear of burglars he could understand, but this ... 'She'll see one now,' he said, and then he sent the weeping girl home to her mother.

Coursework Assignments

Fall-Out

1 In small groups, discuss these statements about the
   story and decide which you agree with.
   * Crawshaw deserves our sympathy. He is the
     victim of his own obsession.
   * Crawshaw provokes his wife, but that doesn't
     excuse her. She's guilty of his murder.
   * It's people like the Stocks who need protecting
     from people like Crawshaw, not vice-versa.
   * It's a story about jumping to conclusions.
   * The moral of the story is live and let live.
   * The writer has got his tongue in his cheek. It's a
     very amusing story.
   * It's ironic the way that Crawshaw kills himself.
     The writer is making a serious point about the
     consequences of Crawshaw's attitudes and
     behaviour.

   Choose three or four of these statements and write
   a paragraph on each one saying why you agree or
   disagree with it. Give your reasons and where
   appropriate back up your arguments by quoting
   from the story.
2 Work in pairs.
   i) Peter Lovesey creates the character of Joan
       through what she says and how she reacts to her
       husband, rather than by giving a description of

her. How did you visualise her? Each write an introductory paragraph describing her, similar to the introductory paragraph that Peter Lovesey wrote describing Crawshaw. Then, compare your view of her with your partner's view. What are the similarities and differences?

ii) How does Peter Lovesey present the story so that the reader sympathises with Joan Crawshaw? As the story develops, what clues are there that she is growing to hate her husband?

iii) Suggest the thoughts that would be running through Joan Crawshaw's head as she lies in bed alone that night after the police have left.

iv) What do you think will happen to Joan Crawshaw in the future? Will she feel any remorse? Do you think she will live to regret what she did?

3 What would the Stocks think of Crawshaw's behaviour? In pairs, role-play and then script two scenes in which they talk about Crawshaw
   i) shortly after they have moved in ii) after his death.

4 i) Prepare a reading of the first section of 'Fall-Out', as you would read it on the radio in a late night story programme. Read as far as the line: 'He had twitched with horror at Mr Padmore's last remark.' Tape-record your readings and in groups of four listen to them and discuss whose reading is most effective.

ii) How would you film the opening section of 'Fall-Out'? Prepare a story-board or a shooting script. Include details of any music and sound effects as well as details of the dialogue and camera shots.

5   In groups, talk about how the story is written.

   i)   How does Peter Lovesey capture the reader's attention and build up suspense in the opening section?

   ii) Discuss how Peter Lovesey conceals his idea by letting the reader share Crawshaw's wrong assumptions.

   iii) Find examples of how Peter Lovesey uses dialogue to reveal the growing tension and deteriorating relationship between Crawshaw and his wife.

   iv) Discuss the ending of the story. Talk about how Peter Lovesey builds the story to a climax and how he hints at Joan Crawshaw's feelings about her husband without openly stating them, so that he is able to get the maximum effect from the twist in the final sentence.

Instrument of Justice

6   In small groups, discuss these questions.

   i)   What is your final impression of Frances? Discuss her motives for behaving as she does. How far do you think she would go to protect herself and keep her secret? If Julia had disturbed Frances searching the studio, rather than Isobel Sowerby, do you think Frances would have killed Julia?

   ii) How would you describe Frances? Here are some words that have been suggested to describe her:
        selfish   quick-witted resourceful single-minded devious law-abiding immoral   determined cold   energetic
        Choose any of the words which you think

describe her accurately. Discuss the reasons for choosing those words and refer to her behaviour in the story to support your opinion. Can you suggest any other words to describe her?

iii) Discuss how Elizabeth Ferrars allows Frances's character to emerge from her actions and what she says, rather than by including any paragraphs giving a detailed description of her appearance and character.

iv) What is Frances thinking as she drives home? Is she right to feel 'quiet satisfaction'? What do you think of the way she behaved? Do you admire her or despise her?

Write a description of Frances Liley's character. Quote evidence from the story to support the statements you make about her.

7 In groups discuss these questions.

Why is the story called 'Instrument of Justice'? Do you think it is an appropriate title? Suggest other alternative titles that Elizabeth Ferrars might have considered and say why you think she would have rejected them and chosen 'Instrument of Justice' as the title.

8 Think about the structure of the story. On a piece of paper draw four boxes labelled The first plan, The second plan, Playing for time and The third plan. Work through the story and fill in the details of what happens in each of these four sections of the plot. Then, form groups and discuss these points.

i) Talk about the twists that Elizabeth Ferrars introduces so that the first two plans have to be abandoned.

ii) Discuss how Elizabeth Ferrars uses the character of Mrs Craddock to create suspense while Frances is playing for time.

iii) Discuss how Elizabeth Ferrars conceals her idea by not revealing what Frances's third plan is so that the reader only gradually discovers what it was, as the events unfold.

Without a Mark

9   In groups, discuss these questions.
   i)   Would you classify this story as a thriller, a ghost story, a crime story or a mystery story? Say why.
   ii) As you read the story, what pictures did you form of Uncle Tom, Aunt Alice and their relationship? Talk about why you formed this impression of them.
   iii) In what sort of house do the events take place? Discuss how the detailed descriptions of the house and its rooms contribute to the sinister atmosphere that John Gordon creates.
   iv) Why is the story called 'Without a Mark'? Do you think it is a suitable title? Say why.
   v)   Why do you think John Gordon chose to tell the story in the first person? How successfully do you think John Gordon creates the voice of a thirteen-year-old boy?

   Imagine that having gone upstairs, the boy goes into a spare room before going into his uncle's and aunt's bedroom. Write two or three paragraphs to add to the story describing what he does in the spare room before going into their bedroom. Try to write in the same voice as John Gordon uses.

10 Prepare a reading of the final section of the story from the moment the boy enters his uncle's and aunt's bedroom to the ending of the story. Present your reading to a partner or a group and discuss whose reading is most effective and why.

Dear George

11   In groups, discuss these questions.
     Did the twists in the story catch you by surprise?
     i)   Talk about how Cathy Ace uses the diary
          entries in the first section to deceive the reader.
     ii) Study the second section. How is it written so
          that the identity of the person in the dock is not
          revealed?
     iii) Discuss how the facts Cathy Ace reveals about
          George and Joyce Melrose in the third section
          contradict what she has led the reader to believe
          in the first section.
     iv) Discuss the ending of the story. Some authors
          would have finished the story at the end of the
          third section. What does the fourth section add
          to the story?
          Write about the narrative techniques Cathy Ace
          uses and how she constructs the story so that she
          can surprise her readers.

12   Write two newspaper reports giving news of George
     Melrose's acquittal, one for a quality paper, one for
     a popular paper.

13   'He got away with it, you know.' Role-play a scene
     in which Inspector Glover and a colleague discuss
     the Melrose case and say what they believe really
     happened.

The Lieabout

14   Write a number of reports giving factual accounts of
     the events that Saturday afternoon.
     i)   The report of one of the two policemen who
          knocked on Mrs A.'s door and climbed into the
          shop.

ii) Mrs A.'s statement to the police describing what she saw of the smash-and-grab raid.

iii) A report for the local newspaper entitled *False alarm* telling the story of 'the corpse' in the shop.

iv) A newspaper report of the raid on the jeweller's shop.

15 In groups, discuss how Margery Allingham tells us very little directly about the narrator. For example, there is no detailed description of her. We form an impression of her from her 'voice' – the way she tells the story – and from the details of her lifestyle that emerge during the story. Note down those details, then discuss how you visualise the narrator and what sort of person you think she is. Each write a brief pen-portrait of her, then discuss what you wrote and why.

16 In pairs, role-play a scene in which the lieabout relates the story of the robbery to a friend. Decide where the conversation is taking place and what sort of person the friend is. Before you begin, think carefully about the way the lieabout speaks. What is his real voice? Present your role-plays to each other and compare your different interpretations of the lieabout.

17 In groups, discuss how Margery Allingham introduces all the necessary details of the setting, so that the reader can understand exactly where the events are taking place. Using the information she gives, draw a sketch map showing the area where the events occur.

18 How would you adapt 'The Lieabout' to present it as a radio play? Individually or in pairs, write the script which tells the story of the Saturday afternoon, starting with the scene in which the police officers arrive at Mrs A.'s door and ending

with a scene in which they ask Mrs A. what she saw of the robbery. Here's the start of such a script:
Sounds off stage: heavy footsteps on stairs.
Sounds off stage: loud knocking on a wooden door.

19   In discussion groups, consider what differences it would make if the story had been told in a different way. For example, why do you think the author chose to write the story in the first person rather than the third person? Could the story have been told as a series of diary entries? If so, how many entries would there be? How would the story need to be altered? How would you bring in all the details of the setting so as to ensure that the reader will be able to understand exactly where the events are taking place?

20   Peter Lovesey says: 'Margery Allingham plots a robbery as neat as a conjuring trick.' In a group, see if you can work out a plot for a crime story which, like 'The Lieabout', revolves around a diversion being created.

The Wrong Category

21   In groups, discuss these questions.
   i)   When you first read the story, did the ending come as a surprise? Had you assumed that the murderer was a man? Did you suspect that Barry might be the murderer? How does Ruth Rendell help the reader to assume that the murderer is a man? How does her description of Barry's behaviour and his thoughts suggest that he might be the murderer?
   ii) Why is 'The Wrong Category' such an appropriate title?

22   When Barry's body is found, what facts about his

movements that evening will the police be able to establish? Imagine that they are unable immediately to trace the black-haired young man from The Red Lion, so they decide to broadcast an appeal on the local TV asking him to come forward. In pairs, role-play the news item in which a reporter questions the detective in charge of the investigation of Barry's murder and the inspector makes his appeal.

23   In groups, discuss these statements about the story. Which one do you think most aptly sums up the story? Give your reasons.

* A sinister story with a tragic ending.
* A nasty tale about two unpleasant characters.
* A cleverly-constructed story with a twist in the tale.
* A murder story with a difference.
* A challenging story that makes you think about your role as a reader.

Choose two or three of these statements and write a paragraph about each one, saying whether or not you think it is an accurate description of the story.

A Blessing in Disguise

24   'It's a very humorous story.'
'It's making a serious point about the way men treat women.'
Discuss these two statements about the story. Say whether or not you agree with them and why.

25   In groups, consider this statement:
'The plot is very simple. What makes it such an entertaining story is the way that it is told.'
i)   Talk about what happens in the story and produce a brief resumé of the plot.

ii) Talk about the way the story is told. What is the effect of presenting the events from Auntie Wilima's viewpoint? Discuss how, by telling the story in dialect, Millie Murray enables us not only to hear Auntie Wilima's voice, but to build up a clear picture of her.

iii) What is your final impression of Auntie Wilima? Each write a brief description of her character, then, in your groups, compare what you have written.

26 Work in groups. Each choose a different section of the story and prepare a reading of it. Then, take it in turns to present your reading to other members of the group. Which of you is the most successful at capturing Auntie Wilima's voice and portraying her character?

The Fruit at the Bottom of the Bowl

27 Briefly, in about two or three sentences, summarise the plot of the story. Then, form groups and discuss your summaries. Try to re-tell the story as a mini-tale using no more than 120 words. Then, in groups compare your versions. Whose mini-tale works best? Why?

28 In groups, discuss these questions.
   i) How does the physical description of the house contribute powerfully to the sinister atmosphere of the story.

   ii) In what other ways does Ray Bradbury create suspense?

   iii) How does Ray Bradbury show the reader William Acton's increasing obsession and growing panic?

29 Why does Ray Bradbury call the story 'The Fruit at the Bottom of the Bowl'? Do you think it is a suitable title? In groups, discuss some alternative titles and choose one of your suggestions to propose to the rest of the class. Then, hold a class discussion and discuss the relative merits of each suggestion.

Twenty-one Good Men and True

30 i) 'The best frauds are only ever discovered by accident.' (page 125) Talk about how the fraud works and the accident by which it is discovered.

   ii) 'Dick Francis's story serves as a warning to anyone contemplating fraud.' 'The purpose of the story is to entertain rather than to moralise.' Discuss these views of the story and say whether or not you agree with either of them. How would you describe the story?

31 In pairs, talk about how Dick Francis structures the story as a series of scenes or episodes. Draw a diagram showing where each scene takes place, what happens in it and how the different strands of the story fit together.

   Talk about how in the first three sections Dick Francis introduces the three main characters and their lifestyles. Which of the three people and his lifestyle can you picture most clearly? Explain why. The story is called 'Twenty-one Good Men and True' but Dick Francis only introduces us to one of Arnold Roper's team. Write another section, similar to the introductory section about Greg Simpson, describing another of his team – either a man or a woman.

32 What will happen when Billy Hitchins goes to see Jamie Finland? In pairs, role-play the scene.

When he has seen Jamie Finland, what will Billy Hitchins do?
How will he set about finding who is transmitting the information? What will he do when he discovers that it is Arnold Roper, will he go to the police or . . .? In your pairs, discuss how the plot of the story might develop, then continue the story by writing a number of extra scenes.

Butchers

33   In groups, talk about how Peter Lovesey develops the plot, first creating and sustaining supense by telling the reader that there is a corpse but not revealing whose body it is, then by the way he conceals the identity of the murderer by setting a false trail. Draw a chart or a diagram showing the main elements of the plot, then compare your chart or diagram with those drawn by other groups.

34   In pairs, role-play the scene in which Frank gives another statement to the police, this time telling them the whole story of what happened at the shop that morning. As Frank is speaking, the police officer should draft the statement. When you have finished, form groups and compare the statements you have drafted.

35   In groups of three, discuss how Peter Lovesey presents the three main characters – Joe, Frank and Percy – by making short introductory statements about them, then allowing their characters to emerge through what they say and do.
Each choose one of them and write a paragraph saying what you learn about him from the story and what your final impression of him is. Then, in your groups, compare what you have written.

You Can't Be Too Careful

36 Here are some words that have been suggested to describe the story:

sad frightening ironic moving shocking far-fetched bizarre tragic appalling

Suggest any others that you think are appropriate.

Then, choose the three words which you think most accurately describe the story and say why.

Write a paragraph summarising your response to the story.

37 i) 'Ruth Rendell shows how a rational fear can develop into irrational paranoia.' Discuss this view of the story. Talk about how Ruth Rendell shows Della's fears gradually getting more and more out of control.

ii) Why does Rosamund misinterpret the motive for Della's attack on Chris?

Write two reports, one in which the police officer who interviewed Rosamund, reports what she told him about Della's motive, the other in which a psychiatrist, who has seen Della, reports what she told him about why she attacked Chris.

38 In pairs, discuss how important it is for the reader to understand the layout of Della's flat. Each draw a sketch-plan showing Della's bedroom, the kitchen, the garden room, all the doors and windows and the side gate. Then, compare your plans.

39 In groups discuss this question: Do you think the story could be turned into a good television play? Give reasons for your views.

Each work out a shooting script or a story-board showing how you would film a section of the story. Then, compare your ideas.

General Assignments

40 As you read the stories, keep a reading log, jotting down your thoughts and reactions after you finish each story. Say what you enjoyed/did not enjoy about the story and what your immediate response to it was. Say what you thought of the ending and whether or not you predicted it. Comment on how the story is told and any particular narrative techniques you noticed, as well as on the theme, the characters and the setting. You can either keep your reading log private or compare your reactions with those of other people.

41 'In the crime story, the plot is all-important. The writer's skill lies in building up suspense, keeping the reader guessing and springing surprises.' Discuss this view, referring to at least two of the stories.

42 Compare the narrative techniques used in two or more of the stories.

43 You have been asked to recommend two of the stories to be read in a series called *Shocking Stories – Tales with a Twist*.
    Which two stories would you choose? Explain your reasons, referring to other stories in the selection, saying why you think they would not work as well as the stories you have chosen.

44 Read the advice on writing crime stories, which Peter Lovesey gives in the introduction, then try to write a crime story of your own.

The Authors

Cathy Ace grew up in south Wales and went to University College, Cardiff, graduating in 1982. She then worked in advertising and marketing for several years, before taking up writing seriously in 1987.

Margery Allingham was born in 1904 and educated at The Perse School in Cambridge and Regent Street Polytechnic. She published her first novel when she was seventeen. In 1929, she wrote her first book about Albert Campion, the detective who features in twenty-one of her thirty novels. 'The Lieabout' is from *The Allingham Case Book*, a collection of her short stories. She died in 1968.

Ray Bradbury was born in Illinois in 1920. He began his career writing short stories for magazines and went on to become one of America's leading science fiction writers. 'The Fruit at the Bottom of the Bowl' is from his collection of short stories *The Golden Apples of the Sun*. His other books include *Fahrenheit 451*, *The Silver Locusts* and *The Day It Rained Forever*, and the short story collections *The Illustrated Man* and *Machineries of Joy*.

Elizabeth Ferrars is the author of more than forty crime novels. Several of her books, such as *Root of All*

Evil, feature Andrew Basnett, a retired professor of botany and reluctant sleuth.

Dick Francis was a professional National Hunt jockey before becoming a writer. In 1953–4 he was Champion Jockey. When he retired in 1957, he worked as a racing correspondent for the *Sunday Express* and began writing thrillers, most of which are connected with the world of horse racing.

John Gordon is the author of several novels for young people including the eerie tales *The Ghost on the Hill* and *The House on the Brink*, both of which are included in the Plus series published by Puffin. 'Without a Mark' is from his collection of short stories, *The Spitfire Grave and other stories*.

Peter Lovesey lives in Wiltshire and was a teacher before becoming a full-time writer. His stories about Sergeant Cribb have been televised and he won the Crime Writers' Association Gold Dagger Award for *The False Inspector Dew*. His story 'Butchers' has been featured in the BBC Schools Television series *English File*.

Millie Murray was born in London in 1958. She has contributed stories to *Watchers and Seekers*, a collection of creative writing by black women in Britain, and *A Girl's Best Friend*, a collection of stories about relationships. Her novel *Kiesha*, about a teenage girl, is published in the Women's Press *Livewire* series.

Ruth Rendell published her first novel *From Doon with*

Death in 1964. Since then she has established herself as one of Britain's leading crime writers. Her books have won eight major awards and a number of her stories have been dramatised on television. She also writes under the name Barbara Vine, under which name she won the 1987 Crime Writers' Gold Dagger Award for *A Fatal Invasion*. She has published four volumes of short stories, which can now be obtained in one volume of *Collected Short Stories* published by Arrow.

Wider Reading

ALLINGHAM, MARGERY *The Allingham Case Book* (The
Hogarth Press)
Flowers for the Judge (Heinemann)
AYRES, HARRIET (Ed.) *Murder and Company* (Pandora)
ASIMOV, ISAAC et al *Computer Crimes and Capers* (Penguin)
BRETT, SIMON *A Nice Class of Corpse* (Coronet)
CHANDLER, RAYMOND *The Long Goodbye* (Penguin)
CHESTERTON, G K *The Complete Father Brown* (Penguin)
CHRISTIE, AGATHA *The Body in the Library* (Fontana)
Murder on the Orient Express (Fontana)
And Then There Were None (Fontana)
DEXTER, COLIN *Last Bus to Woodstock* (Pan)
Last Seen Wearing (Pan)
DICKINSON, PETER *Hindsight* (Arrow)
CONAN DOYLE, ARTHUR *The Adventures of Sherlock Holmes*
(Penguin)
The Sign of Four (Penguin)
FERRARS, ELIZABETH *I, Said the Fly* (Collins)
Root of All Evil (Collins)
FRANCIS, DICK *Whip Hand* (Pan)
Dead Cert (Pan)
Forfeit (Pan)
FRASER, ANTONIA *Jemima Shore's First Case and other stories*
(Methuen)
Quiet as a Nun (Methuen)
GILBERT, MICHAEL *Mr Calder and Mr Behrens* (Penguin)

GREEN, JEN (Ed.) *Reader, I Murdered Him* (Women's Press)

HARDINGE, GEORGE (Ed.) *The Mammoth Book of Modern Crime Stories* (Robinson)

HEYER, GEORGETTE *Behold, Here's Poison* (Grafton)

HIGHSMITH, PATRICIA *Mermaids on the Golf Course* (Penguin)

Eleven (Penguin)

The Talented Mr Ripley (Penguin)

JAMES, P D *Cover her Face* (Sphere)

Unnatural Causes (Sphere)

LE CARRÉ, JOHN *A Murder of Quality* (Penguin)

LOVESEY, PETER *Waxwork* (Arrow)

Invitation to a Dynamite Party (Arrow)

Butchers and other stories (Macmillan)

MARSH, NGAIO *Enter a Murderer* (Fontana)

PETERS, ELLIS *One Corpse Too Many* (Futura)

RENDELL, RUTH *Collected Short Stories* (Arrow)

The Best Man to Die (Arrow)

Shake Hands For Ever (Arrow)

SAYERS, DOROTHY L *Five Red Herrings* (New English Library)

Murder Must Advertise (New English Library)

SIMENON, GEORGES *Maigret Mystified* (Penguin)

SYMONS, JULIAN (Ed.) *Penguin Classic Crime* (Penguin)

TEY, JOSEPHINE *Brat Farrar* (Penguin)

Acknowledgements

We are grateful to the following for permission to reproduce stories:

the author, Cathy Ace, for 'Dear George'; the author's agents for 'The Fruit at the Bottom of the Bowl' by Ray Bradbury, copyright (c) 1958, renewed 1957 by Ray Bradbury; Chatto & Windus Ltd for 'The Lieabout' in *The Allingham Case book* by Margery Allingham; the author's agent for 'Instrument of Justice' in *The Best of Winter's Crimes* by Elizabeth Ferrars (pub Macmillan Ltd); the author's agent for 'Twenty-one Good Men and True' by Dick Francis, (c) Dick Francis; the author's agent for 'Butchers' and 'Fall-Out' by Peter Lovesey and his 'Introduction' to *Thrillers* edited by John Foster; the author, Millie Murray, for 'A Blessing in Disguise'; Penguin Books Ltd for 'Without a Mark' from *The Spitfire Grave and Other Stories* by John Gordon (pub Kestrel Books, 1979), copyright (c) John Gordon, 1979; the author's agent for 'You Can't Be Too Careful' and 'The Wrong Category' in *Collected Short Stories* by Ruth Rendell (pub Century Hutchinson Ltd/Arrow Books Ltd).

Longman Imprint Books
General Editor: Michael Marland CBE MA